# How to See a Vision

# HOW TO SEE A VISION

*Contemplative Ethics in
Julian of Norwich and Teresa of Avila*

Richard Norton

authorHOUSE®

*AuthorHouse™ UK Ltd.*
*1663 Liberty Drive*
*Bloomington, IN 47403 USA*
*www.authorhouse.co.uk*
*Phone: 0800.197.4150*

*© 2013 by Richard Norton. All rights reserved.*

*No part of this book may be reproduced, stored in a retrieval system, or transmitted by any means without the written permission of the author.*

*Published by AuthorHouse 06/21/2013*

*ISBN: 978-1-4817-9769-6 (sc)*
*ISBN: 978-1-4817-9768-9 (e)*

*Any people depicted in stock imagery provided by Thinkstock are models, and such images are being used for illustrative purposes only. Certain stock imagery © Thinkstock.*

*This book is printed on acid-free paper.*

*Because of the dynamic nature of the Internet, any web addresses or links contained in this book may have changed since publication and may no longer be valid. The views expressed in this work are solely those of the author and do not necessarily reflect the views of the publisher, and the publisher hereby disclaims any responsibility for them.*

To the eternal memory of my parents

Alan S Norton (1931-1999) and Con L Norton, nee Collier (1930-2012)

who had the faith to see the vision, the courage to bring it about and the loving grace to instruct me in both.

+ May they rest in peace and rise in glory.

# Contents

About Richard Norton ....................................................... ix
Preface ............................................................................. xi
Introduction: How to See a Vision ................................. xv

Chapter 1: Cracking the Hazel Nuts ............................. 1
Chapter 2: Julian's Benedictinism:
           Paradox, Prayer and Trinity ......................... 9
Chapter 3: How to Seek Perfection ............................. 29
Chapter 4: How to Suffer—and Why .......................... 46
Chapter 5: How to be Intimate .................................... 54
Chapter 6: How to Love the World ............................. 64
Chapter 7: How to Empower People
           and bring about Equality ............................ 75

Conclusions .................................................................. 85

# About Richard Norton

Richard Norton is an independent scholar who read theology at the College of St Mark and St John, Plymouth and the University of Bristol. He later studied Law in the University of Kingston. He has taught in Seminaries, University Colleges, and Public Schools in the UK, Sudan and Zimbabwe. He is a Reader in the Church of England in the Diocese of Southwark, a member of the Mystical Theology Network, the British Association for the Study of Spirituality and a Fellow of the Royal Society of Arts.

He is currently Joint Director of Studies of MONOS—the Centre for the Study of Monastic Spirituality and Culture and is conducting research into the ways in which classical Christian spiritualties influence the formation of and patterns of leadership in "New (lay) Monastic Communities" in the UK and the USA.

*Richard Norton*

He is also employed as Head of Fundraising for an international children's charity: ChildAid to Russia and the Republics.

\* \* \*

# Preface

We commonly and rightly think of "Christian Ethics" as being concerned with thought about our duties, obligations and responsibilities in the performance of the corporal and spiritual acts of mercy.[1] But over

---

[1] The corporal acts of mercy are: To feed the hungry, give drink to the thirsty, clothe the naked, harbour the harbourless, visit the sick, ransom the captive and bury the dead.

The spiritual acts of mercy are: To instruct the ignorant, counsel the doubtful, admonish sinners, to bear wrongs patiently, to forgive offences willingly, to comfort the afflicted and to pray for all the living and the dead.

All acts of mercy, whether corporal or spiritual finally resolve to matters of almsgiving. "The Angelic Doctor", St Thomas Aquinas, certainly thought of them in this way because he knew that the word "alms" is loosely derived from the Greek word mercy/charity) as used by the philosopher Aristotle. For both Thomas and Aristotle the performance

concentration on this has bypassed another ethical tradition which arises from Contemplative Prayer in which ethics and moral behaviour flow from within an interior life of virtue lived in relationship with God, others and the world. It too yields the fruits of responsibilities and deeds.

The chapters which follow will argue that it is from this contemplative orientation that some of the greatest ethical precepts have been given form and substance, and that it is from them that contemporary Christians can reclaim and recover a specific kind of ethical consciousness which mirrors the Grace and Love which characterise the relationships between the persons of the most Holy Trinity. It is an ethical consciousness which is both dynamic and creative. Like the billowing wind of Ecclesiastes 1:6 it moves "round and round" in a circle. But unlike the wind of "the preacher" that very dynamism ensures that there is always something "new under the sun," constantly renewing itself as the consciousness of the presence of God grows, deepens and expands. It begins in the formlessness of silent meditation and is made substantive and "real" in

---

of acts of mercy is not simply a matter of "doing good" in the building up of a just society, important as that may be. Of far greater significance is that they are precepts demanded by natural and positive divine law. Acts of mercy in natural law, for example, are always based on the "golden rule", that we should treat others as we would wish them to treat us. Perhaps the best representation of this is still Mrs Do-as-you-would-be-done-by in Charles Kingsley's novel "The Water Babies which was first serialised in MacMillan's Magazine 1862-63 howbeit that this nineteenth century novel is hardly known to contemporary readers.

*How to See a Vision*

humility, asceticism and active loving compassion. Having received its form in the here and now it dissipates once more into formlessness to draw the contemplative and those s/he loves and serves into an ever closer union with God in order to be strengthened and renewed as it takes shape in our world once more.

This mirroring the interior life of the Trinity in the interior life of the contemplative knows no boundaries and is not content with a morally static universe dominated by hierarchy, filtered truths and our current obsession with pelvic moral issues both in the Church and out of it.

This much neglected strand of what I will call "Contemplative Ethics" will be explored through the themes of Perfection, Suffering and Intimacy, Love of the World and, finally, the Ethics of Empowerment and Equality as they appear in parts of the western tradition and especially in the writings of Julian of Norwich[2] and those of St Teresa of Avila.

---

[2] To write about Julian is timely—May 2013 was the 640th anniversary of her *"Showing of Love."*

# Introduction:
# How to See a Vision

This book rests on the view that the increasing emphasis on "cognition" in Christian Theology in general, and in the study of Spirituality in particular, is preventing us from properly understanding the objects of our concern. Too often we accord a privileged position to the written word and assume that its verbal discourse is for sophisticated people, while discarding the visual as crumbs under the table for the semi-literate and unsophisticated to gather as best they may. We are in danger of forgetting that both the verbal and the visual are equally complex and multi-layered methods of reflection on abstract concepts.

Here in the Introduction I use extracts from the anonymous Cloud of Unknowing[3] and a longer analysis of the Parable of the Lord and Servant in the "Showings

---

[3] Nicholas Watson Cambridge Companion to Medieval Mysticism. CUP 2011

of Love"[4] to Julian of Norwich in order to set out one method by which I think we may recover a sense of the verbal and the visual (using different parts of the mind) as equal partners in our theologising. Indeed, I want to argue that each needs the other to be what it is and that when one is absent from the other both are diminished.

This is continued as a connecting theme in the first three chapters which demonstrate that the recovery of the visual with the verbal is fully consistent with significant and influential parts of the Christian tradition since the writings of John Cassian in the fifth century.

The remaining four chapters that follow show how the verbal is always accompanied by the visual in the writings of the two greatest female writers of the medieval period, Julian of Norwich and Teresa of Avila. They do so by taking the themes of the Contemplative Ethics mentioned at the end of the Preface.

This book ends with a short summary of conclusions from the whole enterprise.

Let us begin then by making a quite obvious point, namely that extant medieval mystical and spiritual texts are the only means we have of recovering the spiritual heights and the sense of the presence of God that they wish to share with us. Their insights, however, are not the result of carefully reasoned argument using the principles

---

[4] Annoymous The Cloud of Unknowing. A 14th Century Text. The version used here is on-line at www.cel.org.cce/annoymous2/cloud.htm

of philosophical logic alone, but the fruit of using the mind (and often the body too) in ways which are creative, open, receptive and prayerful. So it is that the very texts themselves point beyond the verbal and the logical to the insight itself which can and often does seem quite chaotic, even to a specialist.

In the rise of Scholasticism, especially in its Thomistic form, in the monasteries and universities of the C13 and C14 we see an increasing fascination with the rational ordering of all knowledge in to neat, self-contained categories, each part forming and contributing to an intellectually satisfying whole. Yet its progress, leading to a final triumph in laying the foundation for much of the Enlightenment and the rise of modern scientific discourse, was by no means without its critics. As Nicholas Watson [5] usefully points out, Scholasticism had many lasting benefits but represents "a cerebral, academic and unspiritual absence of fear, wonder, gratitude and love." We see something of the awareness of this absence in the well-known contrast between "knowing" and "loving" in the Cloud:

. . . all reasonable creatures, angels and men, have in them, each by himself, a principal working which is capable of knowing, and another principle which is capable of loving. The first gives knowledge of God as the maker of them (the creatures) but beyond that it is entirely incomprehensible. The second principal is Love through which he (God) is comprehensible in his fullness."[6]

---

[5] Op cit Watson

[6] Op cit Cloud

*Richard Norton*

"Loving" for the author of the Cloud is an alternative way of thinking and, like knowing, yields a unique understanding. It is an understanding which adds to and completes that gained by rational knowledge alone. It is another way of apprehending and working an insight towards its conclusion. It does so through using reverence, gratitude and wonder to best effect; using the very things which Watson says are absent from Scholasticism.

This is not to suggest that the Principal of Love trumps other conventional academic approaches to God. But I do want to suggest that we should take the Principal of Love seriously and ask ourselves the following question : "What changes in our thinking about spirituality (especially in the medieval period) if we take "love" as denoting not an emotion so much as a point of connection?" In other words, what happens in our study of spirituality if we understand "love" to be akin to the modern psychological term "affect"?

I suggest that when the author of the Cloud writes of comprehending God in all his fullness through Love it is precisely this sense of love as "affect" (Latin "affectus") that he has in mind. This is made clear in the following quotation:

"This darkness and this cloud is, whatever you do, between you and your God and prevents you from seeing him clearly by the understanding in your reason, nor can you feel him in the sweetness of love in your affection. And so be content to abide in this darkness as long as you can, continually crying to him that you love. If ever you do feel

*How to See a Vision*

him or see him it still behoves you to stay in this cloud, in this darkness."[7]

Medieval mystics often use the term "contemplation" to describe what they have "seen" in their vision and what they are writing about. "Contemplation" is an interesting word in the context of my argument because (apparently!) it is derived from the Greek verb "te" meaning "to see". But it is not just a spiritual seeing. There is a physicality about it too because the same word "te" is the root of our word "Temple" which is both a place of worship (of vision) and an organ of vision in the brain—"the temples"—which we can point to at either side of our heads.

"Contemplation" may arise only because a person loves God and seeks an ever closer union with God, but in and for itself it is not a word about loving in an emotional sense. Rather it is about a certain kind of beholding and perceiving. It is a form of "seeing" with the mind which, in turn, implies insight and understanding which come to a person as a gift. It is the sort of insight and understanding which comes about when we catch sight of something which was there all the time but of which we were not fully aware. It should not therefore surprise us that "seeing", "visions" and visual imagery predominate in spiritual writing and are the very stuff from which the texts take their meaning and significance.

Julian of Norwich uses this understanding of love—as—seeing-as—knowing in her Parable of the Lord and the Servant in ways which are similar to that of the author of the Cloud.

---

[7] Loc cit.

At first, a casual reading of Showings may suggest that Julian opposes "seeing" and "knowing" as two quite different things in her mind. After all, she both "knows" the traditional Christian teaching concerning God's wrath against sin and yet she "sees" in her visions no divine wrath at all.[8] However, there is nothing illogical, incoherent or ill-defined about this "seeing". To the contrary, in Julian's Chapter 51 of the Long Text (her longest and most theologically radical Chapter), we find a precise and logical working out of her theological problem, using the visual to unpack her argument.

Julian had already prepared the ground for this in Chapter 50, in which she gives a vivid description of the mental turmoil in which she found herself in the matter of God's supposed anger at sin. This issue of her conflict has often been a matter of scholarly interest but I want to shift the emphasis away from whether or not what Julian says is heterodox towards how, why and in what ways she describes the conflict as one between two operations of her mind.

She says that she received the Parable of the Lord and the Servant at the same time as the rest of the Showings but did not, could not, understand it at the time. Even though the Parable comes as a direct response to her conflict she laid aside any understanding of it because she wanted to go on gazing at the Showings.

---

[8] Julian of Norwich: <u>Showing of Divine Love</u>. Trans. Julia Boulton Holloway. A Michael Glazer Book. The Liturgical Press Collegeville Minnesota. 2003.

*How to See a Vision*

There seems to be a contrast between "reason", "unknowing", "perplexity", "teach", "tell" "wit" on the one hand and "presence", "sight", "beholding", and "see" on the other. Her logical mind is working overtime trying to resolve the conflict by reason, but at the same time her intuition and spiritual sense are also working flat out so as not to lose the "seeing" by which she is intensely aware of her Lord's presence with her. No wonder, then, that she could "have no patience"![9]

It is not until many years later that Julian wrestles again with the Parable itself and it is worth noting that when she does so she is not asked to look back over any previous accounts of the Parable that she may have composed, but is directed to look far more closely at the images themselves. In each of her two examinations of the Parable there are two levels of meaning. One concerns what we might term the "external details" and the other the "inward", or more abstract spiritual meanings. So in total we have multiple layers of meaning, four in all and this, it seems to me, connects Julian with the exegetical method used by early and medieval scholars to understand Scripture. It connects her with the "erring but creative genius"[10] of Origen, the entire opus of Augustine and, ironically, with the complexity of the Angelic Doctor too.

The Parable of the Lord and the Servant is very well-known and its details need not be rehearsed here. But

---

[9] Op cit. p68
[10] This pithy remark about Origen is made by Denys Turner in his book <u>Thomas Aquinas: a Portrait</u>. Yale University Press. USA. 2012.

briefly, we have a picture of the Lord seated "solemnly and in peace." Beside him stands the Servant ready, willing and eager to do his Lord's bidding. The Servant runs off to do the Lord's will, and falls headlong into a deep pit. There are two aspects to the pit. One is that it is so deep that the Servant cannot look up and see anything of his loving lord, even though the lord is still very near to him. The other is that because of his fall he is so shaken in his reason and confused in his mind that he almost forgets his own love of his lord.

I suggest that this loss of the sight of God is the loss of "affect" in the way I used it earlier. That is, the Servant is no longer aware of the connection between himself and God who is in fact near. Julian then sees "into" the Lord's attitude to the Servant and sees that he takes great joy in the reward that he will give the Servant as compensation for all the woe he has suffered. This is not a restorative compensation putting the Servant into the state he enjoyed before falling into the pit, but an abundant one which recalls that at Lk 6:38, "a full measure, pressed down and overflowing". But this is not Julian extrapolating on the possible meanings of the images she has been shown by means of her reason. Rather the images she has been shown and their meanings are prompted by the divine initiative. As Julian herself says, ". . . an inward ghostly showing of the lords meaning descend into my soul." This is abstract and spiritual dimension was also a "showing" which she received.

Before embarking on the second examination of the Parable Julian sets out at some length the method she will use for doing so. Faced with the most difficult theological

*How to See a Vision*

problem of all the "Showings" which causes intense spiritual turmoil, Julian is told to resort to the use of an enhanced capacity to visualise. This visualisation is not only sharply focussed but also, and somewhat surprisingly perhaps, systematic. She is to work through the details of every colour, of the place, of the stance, of the physical positions of the Lord and the Servant in relation to one another, and so on. By doing so she reaches a point of clarity of a type and depth which could not have been reached by use reason alone.

For example, she had already known that the Servant was Adam. [11] In Adam God sees that the human will remains whole, though human beings could no longer see that this is so.[12] It is exactly at this point that we have some of the most interesting visual images of the Parable; the Lord is seated on the ground barren and deserted, alone in the wilderness. His clothing is ample and its colour was an azure blue. His eyes were black. Within him was a place of safety, full of endless heavens. His face shows both pity for Adam's fall and, unexpectedly joyous bliss because of it. Bliss precisely over the falling of the beloved Son, which is even with the Father.

---

[11] Adam = the first man. The representative of humanity, women and men. The red. The earth. For Julian, it is in Adam that the whole cosmos is met and manifest—just like the "little thing" that appeared to be "like" a hazelnut.

[12] Scholars debate whether, and if so to what extent, Julian is re-writing and reinterpreting the traditional doctrine of "the fall" at this point in the "Showings".

The Father sits on the ground waiting for the time when he can be enthroned in the city of the human soul. Similarly the Servant is, rather dramatically, clothed in a short, tight, sweat stained tunic, "ready to be ragged and rent". The tunic is no longer suitable as clothing at all. It should, at best, be torn up and used as rags. Julian remarks that such a tunic is quite "unseemly" for a Servant who is loved so much. Here we find yet another aspect of the visual use of Julian's mind. However focussed and systematic it may be, it is not in control of what it is going to find and allows itself to be surprised (even shocked) by elements that would otherwise seem fitting and appropriate. At the risk of labouring this point just a little; God sits on the bare earth filled with bliss at the "fall" of the Servant (Adam > kenosis > incarnation > Jesus > crucifixion, resurrection, ascension > us) who dressed in rags: none of these things are what we would normally expect to find in medieval spiritual texts as being "seemly".

Just as Julian saw "into" the attitude of the Lord to the Servant so she also sees into that of the Servant and finds there a love which is as strong as that with the Lord has for him. It is this mutuality in love which connects one with the other. It is their affection, their affect. It is this love which allows and motivates the Servant to run off before falling into the pit in search of a treasure from the earth, a treasure which turns out to be the earth. As he does so he falls "full low" (completely) "into the maiden's womb". The pit, then, is none other than the womb of the Blessed Virgin and so it is that Julian sees a metamorphosis of Adam into the eternal Son of God and this explains, I think, how from this point onwards Julian gives an extended exegesis of Christ and the Holy Trinity.

*How to See a Vision*

Eventually Julian comes to the point where she can say with confidence and precision what each visual detail represents and give them their theological meaning. She does so by means of the verb "betokeneth" which is so common in medieval spiritual writings. So "the sitting of the father betokeneth the godhead . . . the standing of the servant betokeneth travail . . ." and so on.

This verb "betokeneth" indicates that Julian has found a resolution to her theological problem because the two modes of thought, "knowing" and "seeing" have now met, kissed and united themselves one with the other recognising, as I said at the beginning, that they need each other to be themselves. With these two modes of thought, each with its own distinct vocabulary, working in harmony she is able to give a rational account of Trinitarian theology and at the same time speak meaningfully of the visual allowing her to embark on a narrative in which the Son completes his task so that the other two persons can sit side by side. They sit enthroned in splendour, thus bringing her exhausting and strenuous thought processes to a magnificent climactic conclusion expressed in carefully crafted rhetoric—and, by using her example with that of Teresa of Avila so must ours be too.

\* \* \*

# CHAPTER ONE

## Cracking the Hazel Nuts

One early summer evening I found myself watching part of a popular annual series of wildlife documentaries broadcast on BBC television. The programme had already included information about Otters, Foxes, Kingfishers and the much loved Blue Tits and so on, and then one of the presenters embarked on a long apology for the next item which concerned Rabbits. The apology was necessary, he maintained, because, after all, everyone already knows everything there is to know about Rabbits (especially their reproductive habits!) and there was surely little, if anything, more that need be said about them. The item which followed, however, showed that on the contrary there is still a very great deal about Rabbits which science has yet to explore or revisit and which as a consequence is quite unknown to the general public.

*Richard Norton*

It struck me that what might be true about Rabbits is even more the case for anyone attempting to write about Julian of Norwich and Teresa of Avila. The audience already knows, or thinks they know all that can be said about them. Julian is about hazel nuts and if not about hazel nuts then the over optimistic reassurance that "all will be well" despite the empirical evidence to the contrary. And Teresa is about a quest for a spiritual diamond in a Christianised version of "Dungeons and Dragons" played in an interior castle.

All too often this supposed general knowledge is, like that of Rabbits, ripped out of context and derived from more or less popular, and populist, secondary or tertiary sources. Indeed sometimes this ingrained knowledge about Julian and Teresa is reinforced by a vast array of random quotations printed on commercial products, tea towels, fridge magnets and the like, as a visit to Norwich and to a lesser extent Avila too will quickly attest.

It is, to say the least, a very great pity that these greatest of all medieval European female spiritual writers are treated so lightly and so rarely read at length in reasoned, measured and scholarly translations. To do so might be challenging and disrupt much of the stories about them to which we have grown accustomed. It would certainly challenge and disrupt much of the rhetoric, often based on ancient jurisprudence,[13] about what is and is not a moral act or a life-style acceptable to God which is still peddled from many a pulpit and theological lecture theatre.

---

[13] Generally that of Justinian: <u>Codex Justinianus</u> (Codex Vetus) promulgated 7 April 529.

*How to See a Vision*

But it is precisely in that challenge and disruption that contemporary Christians might recover something of the truths of friendship, companionship, intimacy and loving acts towards others which flows from a divine wisdom that comes directly and immediately from Jesus himself. Here we will see that the pernicious and contagious dualism between being and doing, between contemplation and action is erroneous. Rather, being and doing, contemplation and action presuppose each other, contain and express the other in unity. The supposed opposites are not inimical to each other but, like the verbal and the visual, need each other to be themselves. Dualistic thought is not in the original teaching of Jesus and is nowhere to be found in the wisdom he imparted to Julian and Teresa, who from a modern psycho-analytical perspective might be understood as archetypes of the divine feminine.

The problem of preconception is compounded when anyone wishes to write about the practice and experience of meditation and contemplation. Again, there are those who already "know", or think they know, that "mysticism" is about that weird fuzzy stuff that happens to a chosen few whose prayers seem to oscillate between a holy dozing and an ecstasy akin to orgasm. It has and can have nothing to do with them. Then there are others who reject the whole notion of contemplation and meditation on the fallacious grounds that these things have nothing whatever to do with Christianity but have been imported as an unintended and unfortunate consequence of interfaith dialogue.

There is yet another pre-conceptual problem which is the tendency to use "morals" and "ethics" as though they are synonyms.

In short, contemplative medieval women and their visions, the practice of contemplation and the difference between morals and ethics are all easily rejected. They have nothing to do with "people like us",[14] ordinary Christian people and even less to do with the primary task of spreading the Gospel and building up the Kingdom of God.

But what if divine wisdom, contemplation, Christian ethical theory and moral practices which arise from them are the Gospel? What if the Kingdom of God lies on the boundary and interchange between our interior and exterior lives as, say, the "Voyage of St Brendan"[15] suggests, and as both Julian and Teresa argue—howbeit for very different reasons? How might our understanding, Christian practice and "evangelism", understood in its widest sense, have to change?

So to write about the possibility of finding a system of "Contemplative Ethics" in the writings of Julian of Norwich in her anniversary year and of Teresa of Avila a year or two after hers is likely to be regarded as complete nonsense. This may be so even in the academic

---

[14] Which is, of course, ironic since Julian's readers are precisely these ordinary Christians.

[15] There are many modern translations of this work, but perhaps the best is that of John O'Meara: <u>Voyage of St Brendan: Journey to the promised Land</u>. Published by Colin Smythe. 1981.

*How to See a Vision*

community where some scholars repeat the often stated idea that mystics display an unfortunate tendency to antinomianism, amoral behaviour, and ethical apathy.

The dissonance which is perceived to exist between mysticism on the one hand and ethics on the other may be due to the widespread adoption of definitions from previous generations. These definitions are no longer as appropriate for our post-modern milieu as they were when they were first written. Many rely on essentialist, universalist, definitions first proposed by William James[16] and his contemporaries who thought that mysticism could be reduced to highly personal, subjective, encounters, states of altered consciousness, and transient, ineffable experiences of extra-ordinary reality—to the neglect of other aspects of the contemplative's life and the context in which they arise.

In the light of what I have already written it should be plain that I question this correlation of mysticism with unusual psychological states, and the privatisation of the spiritual which emerges from it. It would be enough to reject it as a misinterpretation of the mystical theological tradition but even as a philosophical construct it disregards and is blind to, the overriding evidence of ethical concern in the lives and thought of Julian and Teresa.

Furthermore the field of contemporary Christian ethics focuses almost exclusively on the social dimension of moral conduct, and less on the contemplative prayer that may

---

[16] Especially in his <u>The Varieties of Religious Experience 1902.</u> A great many on-line versions are available.

propel it. It is also based on ontological and theological assumptions, critiqued by many post-modernists such as Jacques Derrida, based as they so often are on a post-enlightenment preoccupation with the individual and the autonomous self. Yet, the intrinsic unity of the spiritual and moral life was central to the patristic and medieval periods, and was even retained to a large extent in the Christian West until the sixteenth and seventeenth centuries in which moral theology developed as a separate discipline distinct from dogmatic or systematic theology. The moral theology of this period "manifested not merely a process of developing theological specialisation but a bifurcation in the inherent relationship of the moral and spiritual dimensions of Christian living."[17]

All of this displays as much pre-conceptual prejudice as anything to be found amongst today's "even-Christians." But closing our minds to a thing, or a belief, or a person which makes us uncomfortable does not mean that they have gone away. Indeed doing so may mean that they clamour for their voice to be heard all the more. This is no less true of what we are calling "Contemplative Ethics".

One of the most abiding strands in Christian mysticism is "contemplation" which emerges from the use the early Church made of the distinction found in Greek philosophy between the descriptions of the soul's return to God through purification (askesis) followed by contemplative

---

[17] Mark O'Keef <u>Becoming Good, Becoming Holy; On the relationship of Christian Ethics and Spirituality</u>. Paulist Press New York 1995 p13.

*How to See a Vision*

vision (theoria).[18] In modern use, contemplation is often associated with "an immediate consciousness of the presence of God[19]".

But if, and somewhat controversially perhaps, we see askesis and theoria as not chronological stages in contemplative practice but as occurring together—purification in the verbal and the visual aspects of the vision—then we might see more clearly the implication that all spiritual persons, all Christians, are intrinsically mystic-contemplatives because of the action of loving Grace in the soul. If we began to think of askesis and theoria in this way we would also see that their referent is a quality of being associated with the mature spiritual life and not simply to those rare, heightened, but temporary moments of altered brain states associated with "mysticism".

At this point it is probably as well to remind ourselves that the Christian mystical tradition recognises two forms of contemplation, the kataphanic and the apophanic. The kataphanic tradition (or way of affirmation) emphasises beauty that is revealed and apparent, whereas the apophanic tradition (via negativa—the way of negativity) concerns those things that are concealed. For the purposes of the chapters that follow, but at the risk of over simplification, we can say that the kataphanic concerns words, colour, music, song and complexity whereas the

---

[18] Bernard McGinn <u>The Foundations of Mysticism—Origins to the Fifth Century.</u> p24.Crossroad 1991.
[19] ibid

apophanic concerns the strange and often unexplained images of the "dark night."[20]

In the early monastic communities, ethical behaviour was the natural outgrowth of both and consequently ethical thinking, morality and spirituality were intimately and inseparably connected. The primacy of contemplative silence in the life of monks and nuns led to "charity and hospitality [which] were matters of top priority and took precedence over fasting and personal ascetic routines"[21] this emphasis on being rather than doing was one of degree, a shift in perspective on God, others and the self that allowed monks and nuns to move from a deeper centre than that usually demanded by life in the world. It was and is a movement into a certain quality of life which Thomas Merton described as the "third position of integrity". Here monastic communities followed a "lifelong commitment to the disinterested pursuit of the good and a willingness to enter a dark night of struggle so that they—and their enemies—might be born again; purged of demeaning stereotypes and liberated from self-aggrandizing illusions."[22]

\* \* \*

---

[20] For an accessible example of the similarities and differences between the two forms of mysticism see the poem by Henry Vaughan (1621-1695) called "The Word"

[21] Thomas Merton The Wisdom of the Desert: Sayings from the Desert Fathers of the Fourth Century New Directions. New York 1970 p 16.

[22] Robert Inchausti Thomas Merton's American Prophesy. State University of New York Press Albany 1998. P92-93

## Chapter Two

# Julian's Benedictinism: Paradox, Prayer and Trinity[23]

The Rule of St Benedict[24] takes those enrolled in the "school of the Lord's Service"[25], that is each of us, on a deep inner journey to the centre of our souls in order to

---

[23] This Chapter was first given as a paper under the same title at the International Julian Symposium at Carrow Abbey Norwich to celebrate the 640th anniversary of the "Showings", 11-12 May 2013. For more on the literary dependence of Julian on Benedict see Julia Boulton Holloway's Anchoress and Cardinal Analetica Carthusiana. Vol 20. Salzburg Austria. 2008.

[24] Rule of St Benedict. (hereafter RB) Trans. Abbot Timothy Parry OSB with an Introduction and Commentary by Ester de Waal.

[25] RB Prologue.

find there shadows of the Trinitarian God and from there to hasten onwards to a broader vision of the One who is Three. This journey is only possible because Benedict is convinced that every human creature is made in God's image (imagio dei) and that the goal, end and entire purpose of our lives is to grow to be like Christ (imago Christi).

This being and becoming is deeply paradoxical. We are made in the image of God completely, but we must also take the twelve steps of humility[26] if we are to find an ever closer union with God. God looks on us and sees that we are beautiful and yet we still need to be enfolded in his love. We are saved and yet we need to be forgiven and the grace to forgive ourselves and one another. We are caught in the tension between the now and the not yet, between the announcement of the promise of God and its fulfilment.

The theology of the Rule is a theology of Hope not least because for Benedict, as for John of the Pastoral Epistles, our origin, our present and our destiny are all saturated by the divine:

"How great is the love which the Father has lavished upon us, that we should be called the children of God! And that is what we are . . . Dear friends, now we are children of God, and what we will be has not yet been revealed. But we know that when he appears, we shall be like him, for we shall see him as he is." [27]

---

[26] RB chapter 7.

[27] I Jn 3:12

*How to See a Vision*

This is another great mystery, a vast arc from creation to glory, drawing us ever into an endless encounter with God, shining, ineffable and incomprehensible.

I believe this to be true of Julian too. So I want to argue that it is this Johannine concept of the lavishness of loving Grace which connects Benedict with Julian and Julian with Teresa of Avila. The first connection, between Benedict and Julian leads me to suspect that Julian was herself a Benedictine; an aspect of her thought which, with one or two notable exceptions, seems to have been somewhat neglected by scholars.

I will consider this briefly and in two ways: looking, first, at how Benedict and Julian share understandings of what Prayer is and does and then at their concepts of the Holy Trinity.

I begin by suggesting that the vocation of the eremite of Subiaco and that of the anchorite of Norwich is the same; to be a living prayer, a perpetual "pray—er" whose praise to God goes on inside and outside the individual and whose day is marked by continually returning to the Abbey or sitting quietly in her cell to pray, and in this way create a continual communion with the living God. Such prayer is the basis on which the whole opus dei is built. It is fundamentally contemplative in character, recalling as it does the saving deeds of God for the whole human race in Jesus Christ.

"Prayer is sitting in silence until it silences us, choosing gratitude until we are grateful, praising God until we ourselves are a constant act of praise."[28]

---

[28] Fr Richard Rohr OFM in a meditation sent as an email message from his Centre for Action and Meditation 29th April 2013.

*Richard Norton*

By this "God is", as Benedict says quoting First Peter, "glorified in all things"[29] because God first reached us in our depths and called us by name.

Or as Julian says:

"Prayer unites the soul to God, for though the soul may always be like God in nature and in substance restored by grace, it is often unlike him in condition, through sin on our part. Then prayer is a witness that the soul wills as God wills and it eases the conscience and fits us for grace. And so he teaches us to pray and have firm trust that we shall have it; for he beholds us in love and wants to make us partners in his good will and work." [30]

Before we can do anything God is acting in our lives on our behalf; and prayer responds to that prior action. We

---

[29] 1 Peter 4:11.

[30] Showing 14. It is interesting to speculate whether and to what extent what Julian has to say here influenced the remark given by Fr. Basil Pennington OCSO in an interview with Mary Nurrie Stearns in 1991:
"We are united with everybody in our human nature and in our sharing of the divine nature, so we are never really alone; we have all tis union and communion. Getting in touch with that reality is our greatest healing. We can adopt meditative practices which enable us to begin that journey of finding our true inner selves or transcending our separate selves and learn to leave behind some of the pain and suffering. As cited in Transforming Suffering 1991 found at www.personaltransformation.com/Pennington.html

*How to See a Vision*

do not pray seeking a response from God. Rather we pray as a response to God.

As Thomas Keating has argued

"Contemplative prayer is the opening of mind and heart, our whole being to God, the Ultimate Mystery. Beyond thoughts, words and emotions it is a process of inner purification that leads, if we consent, to divine union" [31]

God calls us but leaves us free to respond or not. God's action and our response are essential for living a dynamic life in Christ and this means, in turn, that the prayer that is offered is intended to be a vital ( that is, literally life giving) part of the life of women and men.

"And so we shall" says Julian, "by his sweet grace in our meek continual prayer come into him now in this life by many secret touching of sweet spiritual sights and feelings . . . ."[32]

The praying community however large or small it may be, becomes a manifestation, an epiphany, of the mystery of the Risen Christ in the world; the "source of spirituality and nourishment for . . . prayer"[33]

---

[31] Thomas Keating OCSO in an interview with Kate Olson, "Centring Prayer as Divine Therapy Trinity News. Trinity Church in the City. New York City. Vol 42.4 2995.

[32] Showing 4 4

[33] Vatican II. Constitution on the Sacred Liturgy #90.

For Benedict, in praying the Divine Office there is always a clear relationship between the action of God, the liturgy and the rest of life. It is what, for him, the consecrated life is all about. Julian follows this so exactly that for her every hour of every day is, in principle at least, capable of becoming a liturgy which is offered to God as a sacrifice of love. Like Brother Lawrence of the Resurrection[34] everything, even the most mundane occurrence is, for Julian, an occasion on which to practice the presence of God.

This is only possible because for Benedict and Julian all matter and all living things are in perpetual dialogue with God.

For Benedict, God speaks to his people in the revealed word of scripture and silence, in signs, symbols and sacraments. We speak to God with words, gestures, receptive souls and bodies—and silence.

Julian agrees but given the ecclesial circumstances of her day adds that God also speaks in the magisterium, however sceptical of it she may appear to be at times. It is important

---

[34] Brother Lawrence of the Resurrection served as a Carmelite Lay Brother in the Priory in Paris in the late seventeenth century, so long after the reforms of Teresa of Avila and. John of the Cross had taken effect. He is best known for his intimate relationship with God found in the humdrum daily routine of the kitchens and leather shops in which he spent his time. He wrote about it in his book <u>The Practice of the Presence of God</u> and in his many letters to those who sought his spiritual counsel.

*How to See a Vision*

to insist, I think, that it is from her deep, practical working knowledge of all these sources that her Showings arise. They do not, as some populist versions of quotations from her work would have us believe, arise ex nihilo.

The genius of Benedict and Julian is to have the courage to take a range of existing sources and traditions and apply them in new ways which will bring them and others to fresh insights into the relationship between God and human beings, especially in prayer.

There are times when neither Benedict nor Julian feel up to or enthused by the life of unceasing prayer.[35] Benedict warns his monks that there will be times when it is especially difficult, even alarming but that it is at these times that the perseverance in stability comes into play. Monks must face it head on and not run away [36] and Julian too is often surprised and grieved by her own weakness and laziness in striving for an active participation in the things of God and yet has the assurance that "God . . . . keep us safe all the time, in sorrow and joy; and sometimes people are left to themselves for the profit of their souls, although their sin is not always the cause."[37]

Julian shares Benedict's strong desire and a commitment to persevere to such an extent that it is not practically possible for her to make excuses or absent herself from the communal or solitary praying of the offices. And yet this is no mere following of rubrics or fulfilling an obligation.

---

[35] 1Thess5:17
[36] RB Prologue
[37] Showing 7

Rather, the communal or private worship of the Church, which includes the opus Dei, is given to both of them as a powerful means of intimate communion with the God who made them, to contemplate the mystery of salvation in Jesus Christ and to speak to their ever present Lord. This loving encounter is especially expressed, for Benedict in Praise and, for Julian, in thanksgiving and gratitude which, after all, amounts to the same thing.

God's plan of salvation for us as individuals and community, as the Church at large, is revealed in the concrete circumstances of our life in Christ reminding us of God's saving deeds in sending his Son into the world.

Once again we can see here a clear Johannine reference:

"In this the love of God was manifest towards us, that God has sent his only begotten Son into the world, that we might live through him. In this is love, not that we loved God, but that he loved us and sent his Son to be the propitiation of our sins. Beloved if God so loved us, we also ought to love one another."[38]

Prayer opens the eyes of the soul to God's presence and causes it to rejoice that God is so near and all that he has in store "for those that love him."

It is this which for both Benedict and Julian brings about a unity; a unity of the community and the individual with God. Praying in community or as an enclosed individual makes the pray-er part of the praying church, ecclesia

---

[38] 1 Jn 4:9-11

*How to See a Vision*

orans, spreading throughout the entire world. Just as the Apostles and the Blessed Virgin were constant in their prayers after their Lord's Ascension[39], so Benedict and Julian are conscious of carrying on this apostolic tradition of prayer and encourage others to do the same until the kingdom comes on earth as it is in heaven.

At the root of Contemplative Ethics then, is a mindfulness of the praying Church the koinonia, the holy community, which belongs to Christ and has Christ as its head. It matters not whether the contemplative is within the cloister, walled up in the anchorhold, or out and about in the world; detachment from community is impossible.

This spirituality of communion, as we might call it, is summed up well in two quotations from the bishop-martyr St Ignatius of Antioch who died in 107 AD. It might be interesting to speculate whether and to what extent Benedict and, by extension, Julian knew of his work.

Using a not inappropriate musical trope in the first quotation he says this:

"In the symphony of your concord and love, the praises of Jesus Christ are sung. [You should] form a choir, so that by joining the symphony by your concord, and by your unity taking your key note from God, you may with one voice through Jesus Christ sing a song to the Father. Thus he will both listen to you and by reason of your good life recognise in you the melodies of his Son. It profits you

---

[39] Acts 4:32

therefore to continue in your flawless unity, that you may at all times have your share in God." [40]

And in another place he says:

"In common let there be one prayer, one supplication, one mind, one hope, one love, in joy that is without blame, which is Jesus Christ—for there is nothing better than he. Gather yourselves together, all of you, as unto one shrine, even God, as unto one altar, even One Jesus Christ, who proceeds from the one Father as in one and returned to one."[41]

Christ is the centre of all monastic prayer as he is for Julian too. Christ calls them to pray and is fully and really present when they do so. There is something sacramental about prayer. In prayer Christ acts as their mediator and brings them an ever deepening sense of God's Love. He is, for them, quite literally Emmanuel,—God in their midst—who calls them to be open to divine mercy and grace.

In prayer as in the Eucharist we are invited to experience the real and active presence of the Holy Trinity and it is to the theology of the Trinity in Julian's work that I briefly now turn.

In the "Directory for the Celebration of the Work of God and Directive Norms for the celebration of the

---

[40] Ad Eph IV. (To the Ephesians")
[41] AD Magn, VII ("To the Magnesians")

*How to See a Vision*

Monastic Liturgy of the Hours" which was prepared for all Benedictine communities we find these words:

"To be authentic, the celebration of the Work of God (opus Dei) requires that three dimensions should always be found in the liturgical assembly, namely an ecclesial dimension (a community bounded by space and time in which the story of the Church is actualised); a community dimension (all are one body yet each has his or her own place and function); a personal dimension (encounter with God does not happen to a nameless crowd, but to beloved and fully conscious human persons.)"[42]

There is no doubt that the personal dimension is a fundamental condition for the existence of all the others; if this is absent then the other two disappear. The celebration of the opus Dei is intensely personal.[43] Julian's "Showings" are on one level, a treatise explaining how this is so. But like patriotism for Edith Cavell this alone is not enough. Somewhat paradoxically, perhaps, the personal must lead away from itself to the conclusion that, as she says "The Blessed Trinity is always pleased with its work"[44] Only in that way can any contemplative vision be properly personal.

Everywhere she looks, in every passing thought and every hope Julian sees three facets of spiritual growth and desire. When she looks at God she sees three. When she looks at

---

[42] #21 page 40: The Triple Dimension of Celebration
[43] Matt 18:19, Acts 1:14; 2:46. Rom 15:1-7 RB Chapter 19:7 "The Discipline of the Psamoldy".
[44] Showing 3.

Christ she sees three. When she looks at her own life in Christ or that of her "even-Christians" she sees three. For proof of that we need look no further than her Parable of the Little Thing. This is sometimes, but wrongly, described as the Parable of the Hazel Nut. Julian is very clear on the point—whatever the little thing is it is like a hazelnut. She does not say that it is a hazelnut: predication not identity. We will see why that simile is quite so important later on.

The identity of the little thing, God tells her, is everything that has been made[45] it exists because God loves it for "all things have their being in the grace of God"

"In this little thing I saw three properties. The first is that God made it. The second is that God loves it. The third is that God keeps it. But I cannot tell the reality of him who is my maker, lover and keeper, for until I am united to him in substance, I may never have complete rest or bliss."[46]

For Julian, the three-ness in God envelopes all that is in creating love and sustaining Grace. God is her maker, lover and keeper. Each of these three activities become visible, become present to her, in the little thing, in all created things, in her soul. But, of course, it does not stop there. It leads her into all truth as the Johannine Jesus promised:

"When he, the Spirit of Truth has come he will guide you into all truth; for he will not speak on his own authority, but whatever he hears he will speak and he will tell you

---

[45] Jn1:3
[46] Showing 5.

*How to See a Vision*

things to come. He will glorify me, for he will take what is mine and will declare it to you." [47]

Or, as Julian puts it;

"Truth sees God, and wisdom contemplates God, and with these two a third and that is the marvellous delight in God which is love."

This love of the Holy Spirit, as the third person of the Trinity, has another perhaps higher meaning in the sixteenth revelation: ". . . given charity is virtue, and that is a gift of grace in deeds, in which we love God for himself, and ourselves in God, and that God loves for God"[48]

The words "a gift of grace in deeds" indicate that the grace of the Trinity is active within us. We receive the Holy Spirit and this propels, motivates and inspires us to live in its embrace, not in word only but in deeds. Julian does not indicate how faithful Christians should carry this insight into practice in the way, say, her contemporary Margery Kemp did, or as recommended by St Catherine of Siena.

This lack of prescription echoes Benedict's reflections on scripture and the liturgy in which he too saw the distinguishing marks of each person of the Trinity and its activities, but apart from spelling out how and why his communities should be ordered and disciplined as a result, said very little about translating them into the works of charity. Even as the persons of the Trinity share completely

---

[47] Jn 16:13-14
[48] Showing 16.

in purpose and energy, they each act according to their person. The Father originates as the begetter, the Son shines as the begotten and the Holy Spirit moves as the breath of both.

Each of these activities reaches every aspect of life for this too, as we have seen, has its origin in the call of God, proceeds in Christo-centric prayer and the Holy Spirit completes the monastic and anchoritic vocation and chrism of Benedict, Julian and, as we will see, Teresa of Avila.

The unity of the persons of the Trinity and their activities work in diversity and in complete synchronicity, each acting in and through the other, so that for both Benedict and Julian each person of the Trinity does what he is, not that each person is what he does.

In the same way then both Benedict and Julian[49] are careful to avoid being specific about answering the questions "What are we do? Or "How then shall we live?" For them as for the present Holy Father it is enough to know that "The Holy Spirit transforms us. With our co-operation he also wants to transform the world we live in."[50]

And yet, neither Benedict nor Julian is content with a functional description of the Trinity. Their theologies are much more complex in that the roles each person of the Trinity make visible their distinctions so that the one

---

[49] Though as we will see Teresa of Avila has no such problems! How could she if she was truly to reform an entire Order?

[50] Pope Francis on Twitter. 29.April 2013.

*How to See a Vision*

divine activity is completely effected by each of the persons and yet, paradoxically, is distinctly inflected by them.

The Father is the giver, the Son is the gift bearer and the Spirit is the gift; Maker, Lover, Keeper.

As the entire Rule of Benedict reminds us, this truth about the nature of God seeps into our souls and becomes real knowledge which in turn leads to wonder, love and praise.

Julian knew this and in another passage which seems to have a distinctive Benedictine gloss she wrote:

"Suddenly, the Trinity filled my heart with the greatest joy. And so, I understood, it will be in heaven, without an end for those who come there. For the Trinity is God: God is the Trinity. The Trinity is our maker, the Trinity is our keeper. The Trinity is our everlasting lover. The Trinity is our endless joy and bliss, through our Lord Jesus Christ and in our Lord Jesus Christ. This truth was shown in the first showing and in all the showings, for where Jesus appears the blessed Trinity is understood, as I see it."[51]

Endless joy and bliss as a result of the Trinitarian action in our lives yes, but as we might expect by now, mingled with the paradox of the continuing power of cancelled sin,[52] penance and spiritual struggle:

---

[51] Showings 4.

[52] "He breaks the power of cancelled Sin/he sets the prisoner free/His blood can make the foulest clean/His blood availed for me." *"O for a Thousand Tongues to Sing."* A hymn by Charles Wesley in the public domain.

"All of us who shall be saved have within us during our life time a marvellous mixture of wellbeing and woe . . . By Adam's falling we are so broken in our feelings in different ways (by sin and by various pains in which we are made dark and so blind), that only with difficulty can we take any comfort. But in our intensions we wait for God and faithfully trust that we shall have mercy and grace . . . and this is his own working in us. By his goodness he opens the eye of our understanding, in which we have sight, sometimes more, sometimes less, as god gives us the ability to accept it. Now we are raised to the one and now we are allowed to fall into the other. And thus the mixture in us is so puzzling that it is only with difficulty we know of ourselves or of our fellow Christians how we stand, with the strangeness of different feelings."[53]

The question of how is it possible for people to live like that insists on being answered. And forced now to do so the answer which both Benedict and Julian give is by being ordinary.

In his book "Julian of Norwich: Theologian"[54] Denys Turner spends a very great deal of time unpacking just what might be meant by Julian's term "even Christian". What he has to say is, as we might expect from him, quite remarkable. If I have understood him correctly to be an "even Christian" in prayer meant, for Julian, coming to terms with the need to divest herself of any and every theological or ecclesial understanding or privilege which

---

[53] Showing 52.
[54] Denys Turner: Julian of Norwich—Theologian Yale University Press. New Haven CT USA 2011.

*How to See a Vision*

makes her feel special or which elevates her in the eyes of others.

If I am right about this then we might wonder whether if, as we are so often told, Julian was just an ordinary everyday woman, where and from whence could such notions of pride in scholarship arise? The options in Norwich 640 years ago are very limited indeed and the only answer is that she was Benedictine at Carrow Priory in what are now the grounds of the Uniliver building. That does not of course make her a Nun. As Janet Burton et al have recently shown there were a wide variety of functions for women all requiring education and sophistication in the medieval Benedictine family [55] and Julia Boulton Holloway believes Julian was a Lay Sister.[56]

But to return to the point, Turner's point, to be an "even Christian" means learning that we are not special after all. A hard lesson for some of us—as indeed I think it was for Julian in her visions and for Benedict fleeing Rome, if St Gregory's Dialogues are to be believed. Once a person grasps this troublesome truth it is easy, to make the mistake of thinking that being an "even Christian" is to be one of the lads or one of the girls, just one of a nameless crowd.

Turner argues that this is exactly what Julian does not mean. While being an "even Christian" has nothing to do

---

[55] Janet E Burton & Karen Stober (eds): <u>Monasteries & Society in the British Isles in the Later Middle Ages</u>. The Boydell Press. Woodbridge and Rochester 2008.

[56] Op cit. Julia boulton Holloway: <u>Anchoress and Cardinal</u>.

with intellectual or spiritual snobbery neither does it create a herd mentality. Religious pride has destroyed many lives, as the history of sixth (Benedict) and fourteenth (Julian) centuries and the years of Carmelite reform attest, but the reverse snobbery that will do anything and everything to fit in and be part of the hoi polloi is equally destructive.

Being an "even Christian" means being none other than who we are, who God created us to be. And that, of course, does not just make us special it makes us quite extraordinary!

It is not Turner's remit to examine whether, and if so how, Julian's notion of "even-Christian" is another point of connection between her and Benedict. But I think that it is. One of Benedict's greatest contributions to western monasticism was to draw it back from extremes. He will not lay down anything that is "harsh or hard to bear," [57] but neither will he let his monks become too excited either, as the Chapter on Humility and his strictures against frivolity show.

His monks were cut off from the world in some ways, but their communities were also integrated into the wider world. Their basic life-style was simply that of the subsistence farmers amongst whom they lived. Benedict was never a priest, and he envisioned his monasteries as communities of laymen. Benedict's Rule is not an esoteric treatise that ushers its devotees into the mystical realm through the mastery of arcane knowledge and bizarre asceticism. Benedict is no guru! His Rule is a practical

---

[57] RB4

*How to See a Vision*

guide for ordinary women and men to follow Christ perfectly by living in community. As such, its principles can be applied to all lay people, families and every Christian community of faith.

In the same way, the spiritual life of Julian's anchorhold was also not elitist or extraordinary. The contemplative life is a vital and ordinary part of the whole Church. If the Church is a body, then women like Julian are its heart and its lungs, beating and breathing with the liturgy and with prayer which keeps it alive with passion, with the passion which vitalises the whole people of God and makes them whole.

Surely Julian saw her entry into the cell as the most ordinary and natural thing to do. Her visions were for ordinary Christians precisely because she thought of herself as an ordinary Christian.

And that, it seems to me, is the most important legacy which Julian may have received from Benedict: the call to find ourselves, and so God, in ordinary life. The "little rule for beginners" lies open before everyone. It provides one path that leads through the demands and details of everyday life. The family, the school, the parish, the workplace can be and are all schools for the Lord's service.[58]

Since Benedict and Julian know that God is present in ordinary life, their vision transforms mundane existence. Suddenly every moment shines with the possibility of

---

[58] Loc cit

heaven and surges with potential joy. This understanding infuses Benedict and Julian with a great rush of energy, so that Benedict calls on his brothers and sisters to ". . . rouse . . . ourselves . . . run while we have the light of life . . . if we wish to make our home in the dwelling place of his kingdom, there will be no getting there unless we run towards it by good deeds."[59]

Julian also radiates a magnificent vitality in calls to arms in so many different ways that it is not possible to enumerate them all here. But is it not precisely this vital energy that enables St Therese of Lisieux some six centuries later to proclaim:

"In order to be holy, the most essential virtue is energy. With energy one can easily reach the height of perfection.[60] You cannot be half a saint. You must be a whole saint or not at all"[61]?

And perhaps someday scholars will look at what connects the Showings of the anchorite with those of the young French Carmelite too.

---

[59] Ibid p2.
[60] John Clark.(tr) <u>General Correspondence</u> (of St Therese of Liseux) Vol II. Washington Dc, ICS Publications 1988,p909.
[61] Ibid p1133.

# Chapter Three

## How to Seek Perfection

The tradition of Contemplative Ethics which emphasised the possibility of the final deification of the individual soul began in the emergent monastic communities. This early tradition is encapsulated in the famous phrase of Iranaeus of Lyon that "God became man in order that man might become God" (De Incarnatione). Imitation of and participation in Christ's divine nature became the foundation of moral perfection, for it was only through the development of selflessness and a thirst for God that a person could be deified. The primary focus was on prayer and the practice of a virtuous life which was seen to lie at the heart of the monastic life. The whole monastic chrism was to participate in Christ's life as closely as possible and to the extent that the role of the "holy man" or woman in the ancient world was to be a locus of quiet divinity in an often confused, violent and broken society, and for the sake of the people in it. Monks, nuns and monasteries were increasingly regarded as the mirror of the divine in the temporal world.

The early coenobites understood that Contemplative Ethics came about as the result of a deep confrontation with God accompanied by the recognition that a Christian is called to be a living representative, an embodiment of divine love. This ethic of perfection compelled the monk or nun to participate in and imitate the qualities of Being-itself (God) that were revealed in the man Jesus. The path to deification was through the development of virtues derived from Aristotle whose golden mean permitted nothing to excess.[62] Humility was important as the mean between pride and subservience. Detachment provided the mean between the froth of emotional exuberance and complete disengagement and negativity. Chastity was important as the mean between celibacy and the life of a scoundrel and so on. This mystical "method" involved prayer, silence, solitude, compunction, direction, surrender and reconciliation This inner way was for the sake of a higher intention: to be living representatives of Christ's integration of divinity and humanity. Christ was the one to whom all could look for guidance on conduct born out of true sanctity.

While this ethic of perfection did not explicitly address issues of social concern and justice it was nevertheless directed to similar goals and objectives. It was and is an

---

[62] It is interesting to speculate on the Aristotelian influence, if any, on the Rule of St Benedict and why, if this could be established, such influence was lost from other Christian writings until the rise of Thomism.

*How to See a Vision*

ethical code of conduct that marks the life of a monk or nun as surely as moral strictures guide social contracts elsewhere in society. As pioneers in implementing this code monks and nuns also brought souls to God and had respect for seekers of God who like them prayed not only for their own purification alone but for that of every person and every creature.

Gradually this ethical perfection developed an ascetical strand in which the techniques of prayer were employed as a purgative process in order to deconstruct the concept of the self and to bring about the reversal of social and spiritual oppression based on conventional notions of the "real". Far from establishing and legitimating the spiritual status quo, the heights of purgative contemplation were and are radically deconstructive of the person, leading through dark nights, renunciation of egotistical desires and religious norms, and confrontation with the selfishness, greed, fear, despair and worthlessness that grip the soul. This deconstructive function is directly associated with the Crucifixion understood as a reversal of the sensible and the ordinary, in order to reveal the tragedy and exaltation of transcendence. Meditation on Christ's life, death and resurrection and ascension led Christians to reflect on selflessness and self-sacrifice as the primary foundations of all ethical behaviour.

The moral conversion of life presupposed and supported a quest for contemplative unity with God in which the monk or nun became infused, saturated, drenched in divine love so that, in theory at least, any action which was not immediately and directly guided by it was effectively impossible. It was thought to be impossible because at the moment of saturation and as a consequence of it all distinctions between subject and object dissolved and the broken world left behind. Yet this glimpse of the beatific vision, for such it is, must at the same time overflow into creation. Contemplative union is not just a private, personal experience for the individual concern, it is a creative act. This must be so if the individual now participates in the divine life of the Trinity whose circle of love overflows into bringing about a world at all. Contemplative union is both experiential and experimental, experiencing God (if only for a moment) and communicating the love of God for all things seen and unseen.

If contemplation is the repeated and formalised practice of particular prayerful actions within carefully determined times and places then Benedict's Rule insists that every single action of a monk or a nun is to be understood as a contemplative act.[63] From an ethical perspective it is also, strangely, the moment in which what we believe ought to be the case and what is the case in fact come together.

Benedict described the coenobitic life as a school for the Lord's service. The Latin schola is the metaphor which leads his thoughts here. It was a word which was often used to describe military academies in which the students lived under strict discipline in order to be trained for battle.[64] For all its supposed flexibility there is, therefore,

---

[63] Jonathan Z Smith <u>The Bare Facts of Ritual in his Imagining Religion: from Babylon to Jonestown</u> University of Chicago press. 1988 pp53-65

[64] RB Prologue 165.

*How to See a Vision*

something vigorous about living under Benedict's Rule. So it is that Benedict describes the "school of the Lord's service" as a battle ground for eternal life, a battle against the weakness of the body, obsessive desires and waywardness in spirit. Victory in this battle lies in love. For Benedict, it is through obedience, stability, poverty and humility, and through the fear, dread sorrow and compunction that accompanies each of them that the monk will quickly arrive at that "perfect love which casts out fear." (1 John 4:18). "transformation in and into love, all that [the monk] performed with dread, he will now begin to observe without effort, as though naturally, with habit, no longer out of fear of hell, but out of love of Christ, good habit and delight in virtue."[65]

Central to the ritual life of the Benedictine communities, indeed any coenobium, are communal prayer, private reading and devotion, and physical labour. For the moment I want to focus on the first pole of monastic life, as it is the one most antithetical to contemporary pre-conceptions of vital and living religious and spiritual experience. Following St John Cassian (c 360-430), the Desert Dwellers and the Apostle Paul before them, Benedict argues that the monk (the Christian) should attain the state of unceasing prayer outlined in Psalm 119. "Seven times a day have I praised thee" (verse 164) and "At midnight I arose to give you praise" (verse 62) and so on. Benedict therefore insists that his monks (or nuns) meet together eight times each day for the recitation of the Psalms and other prayers and readings. Each of the 150 Psalms is recited each week, with many repeated once

---

[65] Ibid Chapter 7

or more each day. This is Benedict's curriculum for his school of the Lord's service, it is one in which the biblical injunction always to have a prayer bubbling away in one's heart and occasionally outwardly spoken on one's lips is enacted through the division of the day into the liturgical, canonical hours.

To many contemporary Christians the repetition of the Psalms—ancient Israelite prayers handed down by the Christian tradition in the context of particular, often Christological interpretations—will appear to be the dead letter of learning by rote or being bound by the book, rather than allowing the wind of the Spirit to blow where it will. But might not direct and regular contact with the word of God give immediacy to the monk's on-going relationship with God? Is not this on-going relationship often woefully lacking in those "free" liturgies which more or less make things up as they go along and cease with the closure of the liturgy until the next emotional-spiritual "high" can be achieved? Conversely, what too of the monk's feelings in the face of the divine and, if the monk is reciting another's words rather than his own, how can the feelings engendered by those words be his own and so be sincere?

Yet for Benedict, as for the early monastic writers before him, the intensity and authenticity of one's feeling for God is enabled precisely through communal, ritualised prayer and nowhere else.[66] Proper performance of "God's work"

---

[66] The RB also demands that monks read both individually and as a community. Of supreme importance here, and unsurprisingly, are the Old and New Testaments. But

*How to See a Vision*

in the liturgy requires that the monk not simply recite the Psalms, but live them. He is to feel what the Psalmist felt. He is to learn to fear, be angry, in despair, and feel the pain of abandonment and the joy of God's safety, welcome, embrace and love. According to Cassian a Christian knows God, loves God and experiences God when our experience and that of the Psalmist come together as one:

"For divine Scripture and its inmost organs, so to speak, are revealed to us when our experience not only perceives but even anticipates its thought, and the meaning of the words is disclosed to us not by exegesis but by proof. When we have the same disposition in our hearts with which each psalm was sung or written down, then we shall become like its author, grasping the significance beforehand rather than afterward. That is, we first take the power of what is said, rather than the knowledge of it, recalling what has taken place or what does take place in us in daily assaults whenever we reflect on them."[67]

When the monastic can anticipate what words will follow in the Psalm, not because of over familiarity or because they have been memorised, but because their heart is so

---

Benedict adds the writings of the Fathers, especially Cassian's Conferences and Institute and the Rule(s) of St Basil the Great. According to Benedict all of these works provide "tools for the cultivation of the virtues, but as for us they make us blush for shame at being so slothful, so unobservant, so negligent. Are you hastening towards your heavenly home?" ibid Chapter 73.

[67] John Cassian Conferences trans. Boniface Ramsey OP Newman Press 1997. X. XI p384.

at one with that of the Psalmist, then he or she knows and experiences God.[68]

This knowledge and experience produces a particular ethical disposition (affectus) to do something to someone, to exert an influence over a thing, event or another person, to bring about a particular state of mind. Affectus carries a huge range of meanings in a monastic context, from a state of mind produced as a result of the influence of another to that affection or mood in and for itself. Most often it simply means love. The medieval theology which influenced both Julian and Teresa, and which they in turn influenced, insisted that love (with all its sufferings) is brought about in one person by the actions of another.

For Aelred of Rievaux, for example, our love of God and our spiritual friendship with others is always engendered by God's love for us.[69] God acts (affico); women and men

---

[68] Here I am heavily influenced by the writings of Jean Leclerq OSB., especially his "The Love of Learning and the Desire for God: A Study of Monastic Culture" trans Catherine Misrahi Fordham University Press 1961. Parts of this seminal work are now beginning to age and so for a more recent analysis of monastic practice and the formation of the self (which follows much of Leclerq's methodology) see Talal Asad: "On Discipline and Humility in Medieval Christian Monasticism in his Genealogies of Religions: Discipline and Reasons of Power in Christianity and Islam." John Hopkins University Press 1993 pp125-167

[69] Aelred of Rievaux: Spiritual Friendship. Trans Lawrence C Braceland SJ Ed and Introduction by Marsha L Dutton

*How to See a Vision*

are the recipients of that action. [70] Hence the acquisition of proper spiritual dispositions through habit is itself the operation of freely given divine grace that is the love of God. There is no distinction between meditation, contemplation and the immediacy of God's presence, just as there is no distinction between habit and spontaneity, feeling or knowledge.

The affects, moods or dispositions engendered by God are, of course, not restricted to love or desire. According to Cassian the Psalms lay out the full range of possible human emotions and reaction to them so that by coming to know God in and through these affects we come to know both our self and God. While the experience is physical, emotional and spiritual we are said to have passed beyond them to be led forth in the spirit of God with "unutterable groans and sighs" to feel and "unspeakable ecstasy of heart" and an "insatiable gladness of spirit."[71] The whole person of the Christian, body and soul, is affected. They are transformed so that's/he lives them, and comes to know that God is great and merciful.

For Cassian, Christians attain the height of prayer when:

". . . every love, every desire, every effort, every undertaking, every thought of ours, everything we live, that we speak, that we breathe, will be God, and when that

---

Cistercian Fathers : Number Five. Cistercian Publications. Liturgical Press. Collegeville. Mionnesota 2010.
[70] Let us recall that the noun, is derived from the passive participle of.
[71] Cassian Conferences X XI p385

unity which the Father now has with the Son and which the Son has with the Father will be carried over into our understanding and our mind, so that, just as he loves us with a pure, sincere and indissoluble love, we too may be joined to him with a perpetual and inseparable love and so united with him that whatever we breathe, whatever we understand, whatever we speak may be of God."[72]

Although the fullness of fruition in God will never occur in this life, all Christians are to train themselves every day to expect this final unity through prayer.

Cassian's understanding of the role of the Psalms in the monastic life lays the foundation for monastic life and thought throughout the middle ages and so the period during which Julian and Teresa both lived. Many of the most elegant and nuanced accounts of experience and its centrality to the Christian life which especially influenced both Julian and Teresa were the many settings of the biblical texts. Supreme amongst them was Bernard of Clairvaux's commentary on the Song of Songs.

This opens with an insistence on the importance of scriptural songs to the Christian life, not only the Psalms, but also the songs of Deborah (Judges 5:1), Judith (Judith 16:1) and Samuel's mother (1 Samuel 2:1), those of the authors of Lamentations and Job and, of course those of Elizabeth, the Blessed Virgin Mary and Simeon in the New Testament. "If you consider your own experience", wrote Bernard, "surely it is in the victory by which your faith overcomes the world (1John 5:4) and "in leaving the

---

[72] Ibid X VII pp 375-376.

*How to See a Vision*

lake of wretchedness and the filth of the marsh (Psalm 39:3) that you sing to the Lord himself a new song because he has done marvellous works (Psalm 97:1)." Using the language of the Psalms and other biblical texts, writings with which Bernard's mind and heart were infused, he describes the journey of the soul as sung with and in the words of scripture.

For Bernard and many of his contemporaries, especially his fellow Cistercians, the Song of Songs was the preeminent Biblical song. It was the one through which a person attains the highest possible knowledge of the love of God. Bernard explained that "This sort of song only the touch of the Holy Spirit teaches (1John 2:27) and is learned in experience alone."[73]

He called on his readers to "read the book of experience"[74] as they interpret the Song of Songs. In doing so he suggested that in attention to the book of experience the Christian can determine what s/he lacks. Again, the goal is to see the gap between one's experience of God's love and one's love for God and then to meditate, chew over, and digest the words of the Song of Songs so that one might more fully inhabit them.

The soul should strive, Bernard insists, to be able to sing with the Bride of the song, "Let him kiss me with the kiss

---

[73] Bernard of Clairvaux: <u>Sermons on the Song of Songs</u> in <u>Selected Works</u> trans. G.R. Evans Paulist Press 1987 Sermon 1 V9 p213 and Sermon 1 v 10-11 p214.

[74] Provided that the "book of experience" omits all reference to and understanding of the erotic!

of his mouth"[75]. "Few", Bernard goes on to say, ". . . can say this wholeheartedly." His commentary is intended to bring himself and his readers precisely to the desire and ability to do so. Only in this way can the soul ever hope to experience the kiss itself and hence to speak with the Bride in her experience of union with the Bridegroom."[76] For Bernard, the experience of union with the divine, (the "mystical marriage") is only ever fleeting in this life but it will provide an impulse and a motivation for an outward expression of God's presence in moral acts. Ethical thinking and moral acts will ripple out far beyond the monastery or convent into the world.

Central to the discussion here is the way in which engagement with ancient texts leads to, articulates and enriches both the spiritual experience and the practical outreach of the practitioner. "Mere ritual", so maligned by so many in the experimental evangelical movements in the modern Church, in this context, would be ritual badly performed. True engagement in ritual and devotional practice, on the other hand, is the pre-condition for spiritual experience. There is a full recognition of the work involved in transforming one's experience in this way.[77]

---

[75] A spiritual kissing, which is not to be confused with a spiritual one!

[76] Ibid Sermon 3 1.1 p221.

[77] It is at this point that we see that the relationship between belief and practice is far more complex than the simplistic formulation offered by Louis Althusser and others of the Frankfurt School, which has had such a lasting influence on anthropology, sociology and even liturgical studies. Althusser claimed that Blaise Pascal said, "more or less:

Yet, and at the same time, medieval monastic writers insist that this transformation can only come about through Grace. As I hinted above there is no more contradiction here than there is in saying that spiritual experience is at once immediate and mediate, ritualised and spontaneous. For if God acts through scripture, then in reading, reciting, and meditating on scripture then in those very acts a person opens themselves to be acted upon by God. Work and grace, the human and the divine are here inseparably entwined in Love.

Even so, for many contemporary Christians there might still seem to be something of a gulf fixed between the medieval understandings of spiritual experience and our own. Even among the growing number of Christians who understand certain kinds of practice—meditatio, contemplatio, lectio divina and the recitation of short mantra-like prayers,(such as the Jesus Prayer)—as being essential in their spiritual experience, there may still be a

---

"Kneel down, move your lips in prayer and you will believe." Althusser's position is more complex than this line would suggest, but it has had an enormous purchase as an indicator of an almost behaviourist account of the efficacy of religious and other forms of practice. Lost is the sense that mere repetition does little to transform the subject, but rather that one must look to one's experience, think, reflect, meditate, and feel the words of scripture and work constantly to conform the former to the later. See Louis Althusser *"ideology and Ideological State Apparatuses: Notes Towards an Investigation"* in *Lenin and Philosophy and Other Essays.* Trans Ben Brewer. Monthly Review Press. 2001 p114.

suspicion of the particular form such practices take within Christianity and other religious traditions. I suspect that what is at issue here is the association of experience itself, and spiritual experience in particular, with that kind of rampant Individualism which derides and separates the person from his or her community.

A series of common questions seem to underlie many people's conception of what spiritual experience derived from and embedded in the spiritual experiences just listed might be. How am, I to have my own experience of the divine? How can I experience the divine personally, and is not such a desire rendered impossible if it must be bounded within the framework of institutions and in institutional practices which direct my understanding and experience of God? What happens to that part of my experience which I think and believe is irreducible to that of anyone else? There is a keen desire for spiritual experience to be, in a sense, personally owned. But when it is it becomes just another commodity or leisure time activity alongside so many others.

Each of these medieval writers maintain that there is nothing intrinsically wrong with the desire for an encounter with God in Christ to be a central part of a person's individual journey towards God; but spiritual experience, and the ethical thinking and moral acts which flow from them, are not in and for themselves personal experience, but they have the potential to become personal. The experience begins in the community which has a shared experience of God when it is in conformity with that of the Psalmist and other spiritual authors. Only by repetition and greater closeness to that conformity does

*How to See a Vision*

the experience become one's own and becomes part of the continued specificity of the individual soul. To be a true Christian is to share a common experience of God.

Or perhaps, the contemporary concern may have to do with the rich spirituality of Christian monasticism, misunderstood, or at least understood in a very different way. In other words the concern may have its roots in the extent of the monastic life—and the forms of devotional life that stem from it—demands of radical submission to something and someone external to the self. What happens then to the free will and the freedom of the individual? What happens to individual responsibility in matters religious, ethical, social and political that is concomitant with that freedom? Here we see how deep Individualism runs. For here we see that the contemporary seeker after God is not just one who makes solipsistic demands for an experience particular to herself but also afraid of commitment, of handing oneself over to another to whom one promises absolute loyalty and obedience demanded by God, and a fear of regular, repetitive routine demanded by the liturgy in general and monastic practice in particular.

From this perspective, the contemporary debates between the "spiritual" and the "religious", between what constitutes "true" and "false" understandings of scripture and of God, are less about their relative authenticity, sincerity and spontaneity, than about the conceptions of the person, tradition and their relationships that underlie competing understandings of the spiritual and religious life. Must we hand ourselves over completely to God—and to the texts, institutions and practices through which God putatively speaks—in order to experience God? Is this what established religious traditions in their mainstream instances demand? How, if this is indeed the case, are these injunctions best understood in relationship to claims to individual responsibility and autonomy? Conversely, can we ever claim to be fully autonomous and free? Is not the desire to constitute ourselves as "spiritual people" beyond the framework of larger communities simply an illusion because we are always constituted in and through our interactions with others and their texts[78], practices and traditions?

If, as much contemporary philosophy insists, we are born into sets of practices, beliefs and affective relationships that are essential to who we are and who we become, can we ever claim the radical individual freedom that some of our co-religionists seem to demand? How then might we re-think our experience—spiritual or religious, which ever term is preferred—in ways that demand neither absolute autonomy nor total submission?

This is precisely what both Julian and Teresa require. Submission must always be submission freely given. Without the will to submit, one's practices become meaningless and empty. If one is forced to submit by some external means that too undermines the value of one's practices. Yet, paradoxically, both Julian and Teresa argue that freely given submission is always engendered by God's love, just as one receives God's love—and the ever deepening experience of that love—through engagement in

---

[78] Texts are always far more than writings. "Texts" can be understood in a great number of ways as Jacques Derrida's theory of Deconstruction has valuably shown howbeit that his theory is, of course, not without controversy.

quite human practices. This opens up a creative interplay between practice and gift, submission and freedom, the experience of loving and being loved that is a constant theme in their writings and which, in turn, became a central theme in later western Christian spirituality.

Following all their spiritual predecessors noted so far Julian and Teresa suggest that it is only when we understand the way in which we are constituted as subjects through practice that we can begin to understand ourselves, our relationships to others the world and God as we walk along the road of brightness that runs between earth and the glory of God. A journey which enables us to be perfect even as our heavenly father is perfect. [79]

With these foundations firmly in view it is now possible to focus more directly and in detail on the specific contributions to Contemplative Ethics made by Julian of Norwich and Teresa of Avila. Their spiritual journeys towards moments of infusion afford rare insights into the moral consciousness of female mystics. They are examples of how ethical responses directly emerge from unceasing prayer and the experience of God through living the hours.

Specifically, it is possible to trace how, why and in what ways their encounter with God on an experiential level manifested and expressed itself at the experimental level. Or, more simply, how why and in what ways their experience of God led them to a recognition that all life is interconnected and which, in turn, led them to specific social concern for others.

---

[79] Mtt 5:48

# CHAPTER FOUR

## How to Suffer—and Why

The lives of Julian and Teresa were, of course, separated by more than two centuries and yet a comparison of their theology and spirituality reveals a remarkable congruence especially in ethical matters. We can think of them as voyagers of the soul tracing a spiritual journey from fragmentation of the self to self-denial to the formation of ethical principles based on intimacy, strong loving, dignified relationships with others and dignity.[80]

So often the spiritual maps they produced have been contained within the view that they are the result of a proto-feminism, the voices of marginalised and oppressed

---

[80] There may be some interesting and important work to be done in comparing the voyages of the soul made by Julian and Teresa with the journey of a soul outlined in the more ancient texts of the "Voyage of St Brendan."

*How to See a Vision*

women who struggled to have their voices heard in a dominant and domineering male ecclesial culture. This view confines and constricts them, the better to dismiss them. Despite their self-deprecating styles of writing, (or perhaps even because of them) Julian and Teresa were able to take their place alongside men precisely because they worked out the meaning of their contemplative experience and social concerns within the context of the theological and ecclesial structures which prevailed at the time, howbeit that they pushed those structures to their limits. They did so in just the same way and for exactly the same reason as their male counterparts, for not to do so would have exposed themselves to heresy and its consequences.[81] It is for this reason that Julian took so long to produce the two versions of her "Showings" and why Teresa played a game of cat and mouse with the Spanish Inquisition.

One of the many things which Julian and Teresa have in common with each other and with the Church of which they were part is an emphasis on the suffering of the crucified Jesus[82]. The origins of this emphasis which at times became almost obsessive can, I think, be traced to the influence of the earlier Anglo-Saxon "The Dream of the Rood". We can still glimpse something of that medieval emphasis in the many liturgical and musical settings the Stabat Mater. It can be found again in the

---

[81] Not always with success. Julian was prevented from writing by the decree of Archbishop Chancellor Arundel.

[82] The sufferings were not regarded as evidence of his being a victim, but rather as evidence of his voluntary self-sacrifice appropriate to one who is fully human (), a fully integrated enlightened, non-dualistic ONE.

violent and bloody iconography of "Christ at the pillar" and the pious devotion it inspires in so many Spanish churches and cathedrals even today.

For Julian and Teresa it is the face of Jesus that imposed itself upon their contemplative vision most strongly. This is hardly surprising since, as Emmanuel Levinas has argued, it is the case for every human being that "a face imposes itself upon me without my being able to be deaf to it or to forget it, that is, without my being able to suspend my responsibility for its distress."[83] For Julian and Teresa it is always in relationship to the wounded face of Jesus that they are pierced to the core of their being in solidarity for the suffering of others in our world. In Julian and Teresa this intimate and intensely relational love of God forms the ground of their ethics, establishing them as subjects in their own right.

The face of the suffering Jesus cast their own ailments [84]in a new light and led them to identify with suffering humanity, "al christens,", and all creation. In the case of Julian we can see how this identification may have developed in the long years and textual differences between the Short and the Long texts of Revelations. For example it is noteworthy that there are no references at all

---

[83] Emmanuel Levinas: Basic Philosophical Writings. Adriaan T. Peperzak, Simon Critchley and Robert Bernasconi (eds). Bloomington. IN. Indiana University Press 1996. P54.

[84] Julian says that she was near to death when the Showings began and Teresa often reminded herself, and others, that her own aches and pains were as nothing compared to the suffering of Jesus on the cross.

*How to See a Vision*

to the Motherhood of God in the Short text. This is only developed as Julian ponders Jesus message of divine love to her own suffering and the suffering of others too.

That which Julian develops in the privacy of her East Anglia anchorhold Teresa experiences in a much more public way in Spain. Her sufferings are more emotional and spiritual than physical and involve her struggling to come to terms with rejection, ridicule, self-doubt and residual guilt—and all this before having to cope with the suspicion of others that her words and wisdom were not of God at all but of the devil. Yet, both Julian and Teresa arrive at a Contemplative Ethic of integration based on affirmation and on their experiences of divine and personal sufferings. They develop a distinct ethical vocabulary which describes the process by which any Christian can achieve and fully accept themselves and other people as God's beloved. This personal realisation of divine self-acceptance is the foundational to their ethical concerns and of the struggles they had to dignify the rights of those who had no voice in mainstream society.

Julian's story of how she prayed for a vision of Jesus' passion and to receive the three spiritual wounds of contrition, compassion and longing is well known and need not be repeated here except to note that her prayers were not for personal gain, but only as a means through which she might experience God's all prevailing love as her own and to suffer his sufferings for the sake of the broken world. This immediately situates her entire theological corpus in an ethical framework which moves around the core of her vision of Jesus crucified. Julian identifies with his wounds and focuses on the longings God has for the salvation of the entire world. It is a longing, a suffering, shown in his dying love which becomes the foundation of all her theology. Jesus is the matrix, as it were, within which the human heart seeks consolation of sin and a wounding. This led her to develop an integrative Contemplative Ethics based on her understanding of the centrality of love in Jesus' message.

Far from being a desire for personal spiritual gain, Julian attempted to identify with Jesus' sufferings in order that she could more closely identify herself with the sufferings of those around her and bring them too into a knowledge and love of a suffering God. It is in this light that the true meaning of other ethical concerns and moral actions could be more easily assessed. Through the intimacy and solidarity of divine suffering ("for I wished that his pains might be my pains"), Julian recognised that all other ethical issues must rest with compassion which would lead to longing for God.

As Grace Janzen wrote, "Julian was aware that identification with the crucified Jesus must include identification with those for whom he suffered, and hence with their suffering; her prayer for illness represented a willingness to share the pains of the dying in such a way that her understanding and compassion for them would increase and she would be purged of any self-centeredness in her responses."[85]

---

[85] Grace Jantzen, Julian of Norwich: Mystic and Theologian. New York. Paulist Press. 2000. 60.

*How to See a Vision*

In other words, identification with the suffering of Jesus is nothing of the kind unless it also identifies with and embraces the sufferings of women and men as though they too are our own.

Teresa was thirty-nine years old when she too experienced an affective connection between the suffering of Jesus, her own turmoil and that of women, girls, "conversos", and others. [86] During Lent 1554 Teresa had a mystical experience of the crucified Jesus whilst contemplating a statue of the wounded Christ, (a statue of "Christ at the pillar"?). In his suffering she saw all suffering and with it her struggles with an attraction to gossip, honour and social status, being overly concerned with money and trivial matters. She saw how these struggles and attractions increased Jesus' wounds and "how poorly . . . I thanked him for those wounds that, it seemed to me, my heart broke." Her broken heart, like that of the bewildered lover in the Song of Songs, felt the pain of what Jesus suffered and impacts n her increased sense of responsibility to her sisters in religion and her spiritual companions.

This experience is central to Teresa's Contemplative Ethic, because it is in and through her identification with the face of the crucified Jesus that provided the spark which not only put her own life aflame with a love of Christ, but set others ablaze as well. Taking Jesus' wounds deep into

---

[86] Throughout her works Teresa makes repeated references to the dignity of women, social justice and what she perceives to be spiritual and emotional violence in the Church. But it is in <u>The Book of Foundations</u> that her most strident social critique is to be found.

her heart and soul, she was no longer free to act from her own self-will, but compelled to evaluate all her subsequent behaviour, responses to moral issues and responsibility for growth in virtue and perfection against the background of humility and Jesus' own willing self-surrender.

For both Julian and Teresa the transformation of individual consciousness in their witness of the suffering face moves out from a personal knowledge of salvation to a wider social but no less contemplative ethic. The foundation of this ethic as I explained in the previous chapter is prayer, specifically contemplative or, as Teresa calls it, mental prayer. Prayer is the vessel or enclosure within which God's longing for the salvation of all people takes root and grows Perfection and intimacy with God are the source and fruit of the virtues. Perfection leads to humility, compassion and detachment of the soul. Intimacy overflows into ethical concern for the well being of others. The awareness of the presence of the crucified Jesus strives to plant the seeds of justice and love in all relationships.

The encounter with the crucified Jesus instilled in Julian and Teresa a desire to share the suffering of the world and brought them into active solidarity with those who are marginalised, ridiculed and rejected. "I desire to suffer, Lord, since you have suffered," writes Teresa, "Let your will be done in me in every way, and may it not please your majesty that something as precious as your love be given to anyone who serves you only for the sake of consolations. [87] The contemplation of the suffering face takes on the marks of an inner moral compass by which Julian and Teresa steer

---

[87] Teresa of Avila: The Book of Her LIfe 11.12 116

*How to See a Vision*

their actions, and the world's response, in the light of Jesus' loving passion.

In their encounter with the suffering face of Jesus the hearts of Julian and Teresa were torn and whatever traces of ego that remained were consumed in a deep sorrow for human arrogance and sin. Yet this mystical emptying did not remain at the level of feeling sorrow but rather initiated an unreserved sense of responsibility in which they reclaimed their dignity as human beings and articulated a new way of liberation for all people which does not kick away the ladder of meditation, contemplation and holy reading in order to attain it, but rather finds liberation precisely in those communal and individual practices. Julian the anchorite and Teresa the reformer of a contemplative Order, each found in Jesus' suffering a mirror of the world. Through contemplation of that suffering face they developed a distinctive contemplative ethic of suffering born out of many years of reflection and prayer that will now be further developed in the themes of Intimacy, Love of the World and the Empowerment of Equality.

# Chapter Five

## How to be Intimate

"And the more our deeds show that they are not merely polite words, all the more does the Lord bring us to himself . . . Not content with having made the soul one with Himself, He begins to find his delight in it, reveal his secrets, and rejoice that it knows what it has gained . . . And he begins to commune with the soul in so intimate a friendship that he not only gives it back his own will but gives it to His."[88]

In following the path of self-abandonment leading to divine longing, the role of intimacy becomes a central metaphor in the writings of both Julian Teresa. Their identification with the passion of Jesus leads them from mystical union to a deeper, ontological intimacy, which exists between their souls and God. This ontological

---

[88] Teresa of Avila: The Way of Perfection 32.12 164

*How to See a Vision*

intimacy is so intense that it seems as though everything is shared equally in such a way that the soul experiences not just its own will, but that of God. For both Julian and Teresa, mystical intimacy involves identification with God's love and pathos for all humanity seeing Jesus' wounds in their brokenness.

This occurs at two separate but related levels. In the first human suffering is met with and absorbed by Jesus' bearing the sin and violence of the world. In the second this encounter and absorption open up deeper possibilities for communion and oneness. Teresa says that this is not merely a seeing, but a sensation. These things are "felt" ". . . in the very deep and intimate part of the soul"[89] and mystically repeats the wounds borne by Jesus.

It is exactly at that point that Teresa puts herself beyond the limits of the theological tradition she received and so radically departs from it that she was in danger of Inquisition—and may be disputed even now! This is made clear when she says that Jesus sufferings while alive were much greater than those he received at the passion, because "all things were present to him and He was witnessing the serious offences committed against His Father."[90] For those who are intimate with God's presence in the world, human sin strikes into the core of the soul where the person and God are intimate. She reflects on her own awareness of this and how difficult it is for the soul "to see the many offences committed so continually against His majesty . . .

---

[89] Teresa of Avila: <u>The Interior Castle</u> 6.11.2.
[90] Ibid 5.2.14.

that I believe that only one day of that pain would have been sufficient to end many lives."[91]

Yet, the intense suffering as a result of the world's afflictions is also intimately connected to the immense exaltation of love God offer to the soul. The wounding of the inner soul because of the world's suffering exists in a reciprocal relationship with the intense love between God and the soul. In other words the depth of the soul's ability to feel the wounds of Jesus through the suffering of people and the groaning of all creation exists in so far as and in the degree to which the soul experiences God's love. This is an expression of the heights of mystical intimacy which both Julian and Teresa reached in their experience of how Jesus "begins to commune with the soul in so intimate a friendship that he not only gives it back its own will but give it His", as we noted earlier.[92] The communion that takes place between God and the soul in its deepest centre reveals the closeness God shares with all things and the manner in which God shares both the suffering and joy of the world.

This movement between suffering and joy follows the logic of lover/beloved which Julian and Teresa share and in which the "passion of Christ offers a principle for understanding what love really is; it is the standard by which love itself must be measured."[93] The intimacy achieved in mystical contemplation tells both women how the soul in its essence is always one with God,

---

[91] Loc cit

[92] Teresa of Avila <u>The Way of Perfection</u> 32.12

[93] Jantzen <u>Julian</u> 92

despite (or possibly because of) its errors, omissions and sins. So powerful was this understanding of the undefiled love between God and the soul that this equality of intimacy becomes the founding impetus of their lives and theologies.

For both Julian and Teresa the essential self is always one with God. They both use images of fortified buildings: Julian a citadel, Teresa a crystal castle, to describe the soul and write of the outer and inner limits of the fortifications. In both cases the inner soul remains pure and holy, always orientated towards God, whereas the outer soul is orientated towards the world. Thus the outer soul is susceptible to human desires and attachments and so sins. But it brings these things from the world to the inner sanctum and so to the loving embrace of God. Julian says that the best way to think about this is to see it as the difference between sensuality (the outer) and substance (the inner soul).[94]

Substance is our essence, our pure nature created to love God and be loved by God. Sensuality is our response to impulses and attractions that can be overwhelming and to lead us astray and away from our substance. But we should notice this; at no point does Julian think that this indicates a dualism between body (represented by sensuality) and soul (representative by substance). Indeed, there can be no such dualism since the integration of sensuality and substance is the spiritual way to freedom. The integration is the very thing that brings about "oneing", wholeness. Understanding that way to freedom requires mending

---

[94] LT 57-59 290-297.

in the fracture of consciousness of what she calls "even Christians"[95] who feel themselves torn between sensuality and substance and impose a dualism on themselves where none exists and which compounds the fracture.

Teresa too sees the soul as having an inner core which faces God and an outer aspect which faces the world, but her imagery is somewhat more complex. In the Interior Castle she distinguishes three other "moradas" (dwellings or habitations) in which a person confronts worldly limitation, and desire for the four interior rooms of the castle which are suffused with love. Unsurprisingly, it is prayer that is the vehicle by which a person moves within and between these "moradas" just as it is the vehicle for movement within and between the rooms of the castle itself.

Prayer is the portcullis of the castle and is the only point at which the soul moves from oppression and fragmentation to freedom and integrity. As the soul advances in the Grace which accompanies it moves from occasional and infrequent glimpses of the divine into a state of betrothal, but even here "union with the Lord passes quickly . . . [and] in the end the two can be separated and each remains in itself."[96] At the centre of the castle, however, Jesus and the soul consummate a "spiritual marriage" which Teresa describes in images of rain and water—an overflowing of the grace filled waters of Holy Baptism. It is "like what we have when the rain falls from the sky into a river or fount; all is water, for the rain that fell from heaven cannot be

---

[95] It is worth recalling that this means ordinary, "everyday" Christians.

[96] Teresa of Avila <u>Interior Castle</u> 7.2.4

divided or separated from the water of the river . . . The soul always remains with God at its centre."[97]

Here all duality is overcome, for this prayerful union is not the prayer of a damsel in distress to her rescuing knight, of a subject to an object, or indeed of a creature to a creator but rather the fiery passion of lovers who share in the fullness of each other's joys and sorrows. Here even traumatic experiences and physical wounds are embraced and a process of healing begun, mystically re-enacting Christ's oneness with creation in the body. Oneness, interconnectedness, and integrity are intrinsic to all intimate relationships. In both the quiet of Julian's cell and in Teresa's busy Monastery of the Incarnation, intimacy was far more than a passing private encounter with a vision in the imagination, rather it was a fundamental, essential quality of being that demanded an ethical response. In other words reality, the world and its material objects, could no longer be viewed from the perspective of an individualistic and divided self but was to be grasped, borne and celebrated from within intimacy itself.

This, of course, raises a centrally important question: what about sin? As we noted in the first chapter, once Julian had experienced her vision of the Parable of the Lord and the Servant this became a particularly knotty problem and it is probably worthwhile to remind ourselves of some of its themes here.

How was she to resolve the apparent paradox if not actual contradiction between the traditional teaching of the

---

[97] ibid

Church in which "blame for our sins continually hangs upon us" with her visionary insight that ". . . our Lord shows no more blame to us than if we were as pure and as holy as the angels in heaven?"[98] In her vision the Lord sits in rest and peace, while the servant stands before him ready and eager to do his will. The Lord commissions the servant to go to a certain place, and the servant not only does so but "dashes off at great speed" with the result that she soon "falls into a dell and is greatly injured."[99] This physical fall seems to parallel the original fall of Adam and the pain of it is just as great because in her pain the servant is blinded the face of her Lord and unable to hear his consolations even though he remains very near.

Again, as we have seen, Julian explains this in Trinitarian terms. The servant is both Adam and the Second Adam, Jesus, "that is to say all men". The Lord is "God the Father" and "the Holy Spirit is the equal love which is in both of them" [100] Julian goes on to show how and why God looks upon all his servants with maternal love and mercy. The Lord does not blame his servant but understands that the fall is the result of excessive eagerness to love and a hasty zeal to serve. For Julian then, sin is negative only insofar as and in the degree to which it results from a misunderstanding of what it is to truly love. Sin is an absence of that true love and this might recall Augustine's of Hippo's suggestion that evil is privatio boni—an absence or obverse of good. According to Julian this is exactly how God regards our sins: "and then I saw

---

[98] Showing 50
[99] Showing 51
[100] Ibid 274

that only pain blames and punishes, and our courteous Lord comforts and succours, and always he is kindly disposed to the soul, loving and longing to bring it to bliss"[101] This becomes for Julian the central message of the doctrines of the incarnation and the Trinity—evil and sin are transformed through love

It is in this sense that Julian's theology shares with some of the Fathers of the late antique era a quest for integration, a union of the fragmented tripartite human self into wholeness which, in turn teaches us about the interconnectedness of the world and the nature of bodies both human and divine in relation to it.[102] Like those early Fathers this interconnectedness, this intimacy, provides Julian with a framework of guidelines for the human ethical response to evil and sin. She describes not by extending the image of lord and servant, which may be a masculine trope, but between a child and his mother, between Jesus and Mary his mother; a distinct and deliberately chosen feminine image.

For Liz McAvoy it is only through the filter of the more feminine imagery that it is possible to understand the image of the vision of the Lord and servant at all. She wrote:

"Julian presents the mother-figure as the one who feels in her own body every hurt her child receives, both physical

---

[101] Ibid 271
[102] Hannah Hunt <u>Clothed in the Body—Asceticism, the Body and the Spiritual in the Late Antique Era.</u> Ashgate. UK. July 2012.

and psychological, and so this lord feels the suffering of his servant and is united with him in his anguish. The pain of the fall unites them both, just as the pin of childbirth and the suffering involved in the child's acquisition of experience unites mother and child in a continuous cycle of reciprocity. The resultant effect of the feminisation of language is the disruption of traditional masculine absolutism embedded in the concept of vengeance and the assertion of nurturing values of the maternal feminine both in a human and divine context as a solution to the problem."[103] According to Constance Fitzgerald this disruption led, in turn, to a deeper understanding of God's pathos for human affliction and suffering. For her, this is "the point in life and prayer development [when] the images of the poor, the victimised, the oppressed, the exploited, and the suffering take on a clarity and significance which is overpowering"[104]

This is the context in which God's telling Julian that "all will be well" must be understood. God loves the world, suffers over it, for it and with it, and desires that all will be well. That all things will be well is a function of God's loving presence and not, as so often and mistakenly argued,

---

[103] Liz Herbert McAvoy The Moders Service: Motherhood as matrix in Julian of Norwich Mystics Quarterly 24 1998. 4 192

[104] Constance Fitzgerald Transformation in Wisdom: The Subversive Character and Educative Power of Sophia in Contemplation. In Carmel and Contemplation: Transforming Human Consciousness. Keviin Culligan and Regis Jordan (eds). Washington DC: institute of Carmelite Studies 2000, 311 and 314.

a function of human aspiration in the face of counter factual evidence that things are far from well—however Christian they may be. In so far as and in the degree to which human beings participate in this divine desire it is a participation in God's witness, a seeing of the world from God's perspective that subverts and contradicts the whole individual perception of reality.

So it is that the ethics of intimacy lead to healing and an active desire both to heal the suffering of others and to lift up the collective longing and pain of humanity, bringing each and all to a deep knowledge of divine love. Teresa has much to say on this particular point and writes of how God showed her the experience of hell with the specific purpose of helping her to understand the urgency of making an ethical response and moral actions in healing spiritual wounds. She wrote:

"I notice that if we see a person . . . with a great trial or suffering, it seems that our very own nature invites us to compassion; and if their trial is great, we ourselves become distressed . . . No heart can bear it without great pain . . . this awareness also makes me desire that in a matter so important we don't grow satisfied with anything less than doing all we can on our part; let us neglect nothing, and may it please the Lord that he be served by giving us the grace to do all that we can."[105]

Intimacy creates an ethic of mutuality and compassion, a desire to share in and bring healing to the sorrows of others.

---

[105] Teresa of Avila Life 32.6

# CHAPTER SIX

## How to Love the World

"At the same time as I saw this sight of the head bleeding, our good Lord showed a spiritual sight of his familiar love. I saw that he is to us everything which is good and comforting for our help. He is our clothing, who wraps and enfolds us for love, embraces and shelters us, surrounds us for his love, which is so tender that he may never desert us. And so in this sight I saw that he is everything which is good, as I understand."[106]

Julian's first vision accounts for nine chapters in the so-called "Long Text." It is a showing ( demonstration) of divine love in which all that follows from it is "founded and connected."[107] In a commentary on "his precious

---

[106] Showing 5
[107] Showing 1

crowning of thorns"[108] Julian uses these chapters to express the union between God and the soul and the joy to be found in understanding the Trinity as "our maker . . . our protector, and our everlasting lover,"[109] and the familiar love in which God enfolds and embraces all creation. While the vision is that of Jesus' bloodied head, the theology which emerges from it is one of healing, flourishing and loving the world.

Julian repeatedly emphasises her understating that God wraps all things in his love, caring for even the smallest of them and so the minutiae of our existence, so that "we, soul and body, [are] clothed and enclosed in his goodness."[110] Her insistence is plainly intended to bring about a different view of the world, an amor mundi or love of the world. The similarities between Julian's concept of amor mundi and that explored in the works of Hannah Arendt et al are quite remarkable to the extent that, perhaps, one has influenced the other.[111]

The ethic of the love of the world has its primary focus on the ways in which people might fully realise their potential as individuals in community and as children of God.

---

[108] ibid

[109] Showing 4

[110] Showing 6

[111] James W Bernauer (ed) <u>Amor Mundi: Explorations in the Faith and thought of Hannah Arendt</u>. Boston. Martinous Nijoff Publishers 1987. Grace Jantzen has a detailed account of Arendt's concept of in her book: <u>Becoming Divine:Towards a Feminist Philosophy of Religion</u> chapter 6. Manchester University Press 1998.

*Richard Norton*

The communal aspect is particularly important since, for Julian, it is a counterbalance to the tendency to privatise and spiritualise moral conduct. It is for this reason that she controversially maintained that ethical principles were derived from God's love, holding and sustaining all things in being, rather than from theological or metaphysical doctrines.[112] The world "lasts and always will because God loves it."[113]

It is this that forms the framework within which Julian's famous image of the hazelnut is to be understood and apart from which it makes almost no sense. For here in this first revelation Julian creatively juxtaposes the bleeding and suffering head of Jesus with a tiny object the size of which is "no bigger than a hazelnut"[114] which she can easily hold on the palm of her hand. That it exists at all is an expression of God's love. God's love is at the centre of its being sustaining and nourishing it.

So it is with people. That people exist is an expression of God's love and because human beings are uniquely able to respond to and reciprocate love. It is for love that human beings are created. God's love, whether we welcome it and are consciously aware of it or not, is at the very core of our being. Even though God delights in the human capacity to respond in love his divine love is neither conditional

---

[112] Jantzen <u>Becoming Divine</u> 153

[113] Showing 8

[114] Once again, it is important to emphasise that Julian is writing about actual hazelnuts, but comparing an as yet undefined and unknown tiny object to something more familiar, a hazelnut. It is a trope, not identification.

*How to See a Vision*

upon nor restricted by the human response.[115] Divine love grows and overflows from the hearts of those kept in the palm of God's hands towards others, seeking them and surrounding them with love, the more so if human love is joined with it. Julian describes it in this way:

"I was greatly moved in love towards my fellow Christians, that they might see and know what I saw, for I wished it to be a comfort to them, for all this vision was shown for all men."[116]

This loving concern leads directly into another of Julian's major themes which, like that of the image of the hazelnut is frequently misunderstood; her concept of the motherhood of God. This too is a trope or rather a paradigm or model in which, according to McAvoy, she has come to recognise the crucial nature of the feminine, particularly of the maternal, to the understanding of God's love for humanity and his attitude towards sin, and for her, the divine and the feminine are inseparable.[117]

But this neither implies nor entails that God is feminine any more than God is masculine, for God is beyond gender in this sense. What Julian sees is that just as objects and people are held in and by God's love so are their "accidental" predicates and distinguishing qualities. This too is important because it further roots, grounds, embodies and makes physical God's love for all created things. God's love is tangible and this, in turn, has an

---

[115] Or their sexual preferences and practices either.
[116] LT 8 190
[117] Mc Avoy <u>The Moders Service</u> 193

enormous impact on Julian's soteriology,[118] howbeit that this was not fully developed for another fifteen years during which she must have been aware of the devastation of the Black Death and the many political and social upheavals of those years.

In 1388 Julian began to ponder the meaning of these events in the light of her showings. She set both against her understanding that "all would be well and every kind of thing would be well."[119] How could this be, where might the truth lie for these years so marked by suffering and sin? It was a question which remained with her until the closing chapter of the Long Text and the answer she received was that it was all a matter of love. This is often taken to be the high point of Julian's narrative and on one level it is. But it may equally be regarded as being as evasive as God's words to Job at the end of his suffering. An alternative reading of what Julian writes might make this clear:

"After fifteen years and more, I was answered in spiritual understanding, and it was said: What, do you wish to know the Lord's meaning in this thing? Know it well, love was his meaning. Who reveals it to you? Love. What did he reveal to you? Love. Why does he reveal it to you? Love. For Love . . . And so I was taught that Love is our Lord's meaning."

---

[118] Loc cit and LT 60 297
[119] For further analysis see Jantzen <u>Julian</u> chapter 1 and <u>Showing 13.</u>

*How to See a Vision*

It is surely possible to detect a note of weariness and frustration in the first sentence which is answered by a question which seems to suggest that Julian is more than a little presumptive to even voice her desire to know the meaning of these years. A substitution of an exclamation mark for the comma would indicate something of this. Then the words "know well" can also be read as a stern warning against presumption as if to a small child as in "Look, I'm going to say this only once . . ."

From that point on God who is a parent almost mimics and ridicules her questioning giving the same oft repeated answer.

It may have been a very long time indeed before Julian was able to write the next sentence which might also be read as though she is doing so in a spirit of surrender:

"And I saw very clearly in this and in everything that before God made us he loved us, which love was never abated and never will be."[120]

If I am right about this alternative reading, or at least emphasis on the words of this final statement what is to be made of it? Simply this, that however much a person may feel and be surrounded and protected by God loving presence there is still an actual and epistemological distance between creator and creatures, a distance which cannot and must not be crossed even in thought without peril. God and people although in intimate and inseparable

---

[120] Showing 86.

relationship are nevertheless two quite different states of being.

Julian's amor mundi then is complex. It allows for human and divine compassionate grace to be shown to all creatures and even to inanimate objects in love. The love of which she writes might be salvific but it is never sentimental. It might be the means by which God reconciles all things to himself. But the love of which she writes never denies, belittles or attempts to sweep away the pain the hurt and the anguish of suffering. It is not a love which is counter-factual, whistling in the dark against all that would count against it. It is never merely passive, a sort of Christian comfort blanket in which we can wrap ourselves up close our eyes and try to convince ourselves that all will be well when it jolly well isn't. No, for this love is costly and always with remainder and that is On the contrary, it is a revolutionary cry, a call to arms, as serious and as heartfelt as Lenin's question "What is to be done?" [121]

If Lenin called for proletarian activism as a means out of their oppression, how much more might it be the case that Julian saw that the whole world might be transformed when "even Christians" rally to the cause of love—the standard of which is Jesus' suffering love on Calvary?

We can find a similarly complex amor mundi in the writings of Teresa of Avila and like that of Julian, though

---

[121] Vladimir Ilyich Lenin What is to be Done?—Burning Questions of our Movement in Lenin's Collected Works. Volume 5. Joe Fineberg and George Hanna (trans) Foreign Language Publishing House Moscow 1961. 347-530.

*How to See a Vision*

for different reasons, it is born of struggle. Teresa struggled with an overwhelming sense of God's love and her own unworthiness to receive it. Perez-Romero suggests that Teresa's sense of unworthiness came from two interconnected sources, her inner lack of self-confidence and the role of women in sixteenth century Spain.[122] I am not entirely convinced by this because it does not explain how it is that in writing about her self-struggle Teresa means us to see in it the fractured existence of those who neither loved nor love. If Teresa suffered from a lack of self concept we might expect her concern to be with herself and her own wants, desires and needs—but it never is.[123] Her concern, like that of Julian, is always for others and the development of their spiritual relationship with God played out in the practical hustle and bustle of the world bringing about a reconciliation of the divine and the temporal through love. Like Julian too she learns that God's all-embracing love first cherishes and empowers herself, then her fellow Carmelites and their surrounding communities and then overflows to encompass all things and all people. [124]

Teresa finds this love in the depth of her soul where she is united with God. But this unity is not passive but equips

---

[122] Antonio Perez-Romero: Subversion and Liberation in the Writings of St Teresa of Avila Amsterdam and Atlanta. Rodolphi Press 1996

[123] Perez-Romero must also explain Teresa's insistence at Way of Perfection 65-66 that the love she experiences and shows has "no self-interest at all"

[124] It is important to give a close reading of the entire to understand the depth of this struggle.

her with energy and a desire for all people to experience the same union. Her entire mission and ministry were to find ways in which that union would become possible for everyone with whom she came into contact. For Teresa only an overwhelming sense of interior Love can provide a secure basis from which to conduct external acts of compassion. She wrote:

"Once while I was reciting with all the Sisters the hours of the divine office my soul suddenly . . . seemed to me to be like a polished mirror . . . in its centre Christ, our Lord, was shown to me . . . as though in a mirror. And this mirror also . . . was completely engraved upon the Lord himself by means of a very loving communion I would not know how to describe."[125]

This love cannot be kept as a treasure of her own but compels her to the essential work of compassion for others and the whole created order. It is a love which has "no self-interest at all" because it reflects the love "which the good lover Jesus had for us"[126] Just as it cannot be kept so this love is not unconcerned or detached from the progress

---

[125] Teresa of Avila: Life 356. It may also be useful to remember that while glass mirrors were available in the late Middle Ages they were something of a luxury. Most mirrors were much as they had been since the Roman period and made of metal. Where glass mirrors could be afforded the glass was of somewhat inferior quality especially when compared to modern glass. It needed to be polished very regularly in order for them to reflect at all. Without doing so a person would, at best, see only darkly. (1. Cor 13.12)

[126] Teresa of Avila: The Way of Perfection 65-66

of another person in love. Rather, and to the contrary, this love is extremely costly demanding nothing less than that she is entirely spent in its extension and cause. It is costly too for those who receive it, for it causes spiritual pain in prayer, in tears, in penances and other disciplined spiritual practices. But precisely in that suffering love they will find consolation enough to make progress in true love so that when a person is pierced by the hot arrow of love they will "do everything he can for the other's benefit; he will lose a thousand lives that a little good might come to the other soul. O precious love that imitates the commander-in-chief of love, Jesus our Good!"[127]

For Teresa as for Julian, Jesus suffered from love, human beings are made in the image of God, holy, blameless and loving (Ephesians 1:4) and our sins are redeemed through love. Ethical thought and moral behaviour flow from this divine love in a torrent of desire. It is a basic, foundational, love enfolding all creatures in its embrace but unleashing pure thought and action. This amor mundi produces well-being and wholeness, personal flourishing and finds it highest point in the cycle of birth, growth and replenishment which brings forth the astonishing diversity of all that is. It is this loving cycle which propels the world towards its fullest potential and enables it to fulfil it. [128]

This love lies at the very heart of God. It is the means by which God in Christ reconciles all things to himself. (2.Cor 15:19). It is love that makes sin so painful, not punishment. Love cannot cope with the punishment of

---

[127] Ibid 65
[128] Jantzen <u>Becoming Divine</u> Chapter 6

the lover. It is for Teresa and Julian a maternal love, healing the fractures of consciousness that wounds love and out of this understanding both women give a call to humility and devotion as the surest response to that love and as the clearest sign of Grace.

The ethic of amor mundi therefore gives a useful corrective to those who read both Julian and Teresa as being preoccupied, even obsessed with the salvation of the individual soul. It was not individual freedom which they sought alone, but their desire to use freedom in the service of others. If one thing distinguishes these two feminine mystics it is surely this intense compassion for the longing and the pains of others, among them their sisters in religion, neighbours, clergy, friends and strangers alike. Infused throughout their texts, even in the rhetoric of dispassion, frustration and even anger at certain human actions in the world, is the importance of loving the world into being, celebrating its very existence and working to mend the fractures in consciousness and in communities through love. In short the contemplative ethic of loving the world can be summed up in the words of Teresa "The important thing is not to think much, but to love much"[129]

---

[129] Terersa of Avila <u>Interior Castle</u> 319

# Chapter Seven

# How to Empower People and bring about Equality

We come now, finally, to an issue which haunts the works of Julian and Teresa which is not present, or at least not in the same way, in other medieval feminine theologians. It is the question of whether they wrote from a wholly or largely feminine perspective and, if they did, to what extent was this deliberate confrontation to the ecclesial authority of their day? In short, to what extent might their writings be regarded as a manifesto for the empowerment of women then and now?

It is sometimes supposed that the cultural and ecclesial arrangements of the High Middle Ages were at best suspicious of and at worst inimical to women in general and women religious in particular. This generalisation is so entrenched as to be almost an a priori truth so that

Julian and Teresa's writings are read as though they were nothing but a means of confronting their subordination and disempowerment as women. It is this which is said to be the most enduring and important quality of their work, revealing the deep wounds, spiritual and emotional, that a masculine society and Church can (and does) inflict on those whom it marginalises simply because they are of a different gender.

Well . . . perhaps. But is not this stance equally disempowering? Does it not assume that were the High Middle Ages not as oppressive of women as it is believed, that these women would have nothing to say? Does it not assume that what Julian and Teresa have to say is reactive to their own social conditions rather than proactive in the cause of the Gospel and the Kingdom of God? Does it not overlook and equally marginalise their theology which at once transcends all social arrangements and yet is addressed and applicable to them?

From the previous chapters it should be plain that I do not think it possible to confine either Julian or Teresa to their contemporary context any more than we would wish to do with the theologies of Augustine of Hippo or the Angelic Doctor. The age in which they wrote might at some level be both interesting and useful in providing a key to the unlocking of some concepts and language which are now lost to us. But there is in Julian and Teresa, as for Augustine and Thomas, a series of timeless truths which flow from a central understanding of the Christian life which they all equally share: namely, that the goal of the Christian life is theosis. In the process of theosis Julian and Teresa accepted their self-worth and dignity before God

*How to See a Vision*

To be one with God, united with him without loss of identity was something for which both Julian and Teresa earnestly prayed so that anything and everything which impedes the progress of a soul towards God is unethical, as the previous essays have endeavoured to show. If the contemplative ethic of perfection provided the engine of their longing for unity so the amor mundi culminates in an ethic of dignity for all things. To love as God loves requires a healing of the wounds that fracture and divide a society and individuals against themselves. As the poet Auden wrote:

"In the desert of the heart
Let the healing fountains start;
In the prison of his days
Teach the free man how to praise . . ."[130]

During the period between the writing of her Short and Long Texts—"the prison of her days"—Julian felt "the healing fountains start" in such a way that the language of harsh self-criticism was greatly reduced, In its place we see a greater sense of personal authority as a woman and as a female mystical theologian. In the Short text Julian suggests that her writings are those of a "wretched worm, the sinful creature to whom it [revelation] was shown."[131] In the corresponding passage in the long Text, however, the language is radically changed and its self-deprecating tone eliminated. It still speaks of her human frailty, weakness and ignorance but she is now able to assert that

---

[130] W.H.Auden: <u>In Memory of W B Yates.</u> As quoted at <u>www.poets.org/viewmedia.php</u>

[131] ST 6 133

". . . because I am a woman, ought I therefore to believe that I should not tell you of the goodness of God?"[132] This is, I think, illustrative of the importance Julian places on empowerment which comes from Contemplative Ethics.

This sense of empowerment as a woman and as a female theologian-mystic is which comes from the Ethics derived from contemplation is, however, seen much more easily in the writings of Teresa of Avila. Her radical reinterpretations of the role of women and, perhaps, the unique character of female spirituality, grows in due proportion with her intimacy with God. As she progresses in the spiritual journey, Teresa confronts a deeper and more radical fracture which inhabits her consciousness and battles to first recognise and then attempt to defeat the misogyny of her age which has so greatly damaged her self-concept.

This fracturing is made plain by her frustration caused by the assaults on her spiritual life by powerful male confessors and advisors who seem to have been intent on keeping her subordinated. In the light of our contemporary knowledge of psychology it may be that this suppression speaks more about the insecurity of the confessors in feeling threatened by her than about Teresa herself. The extent to which this may or may not be true does not detract from the fact that according to their existing theology that of Teresa pressed hard against the boundaries of heresy. Some thought it was demonic.[133] Spiritual domination, which undergirded the

---

[132] Ibid 135
[133] For an excellent contemporary analysis of the issue, see Kathleen Fischer; <u>Violence against Women—the spiritual dimension</u> in Kathleen Fischer, <u>Women at the</u>

economic and social milieu of her day and contributed to the further marginalisation of women created hidden scars in Teresa's soul—scars that could only be healed as she learnt to map the contemplative process that took her through what might be thought of as the "dark night of the feminine" and into the blinding love of dignity and intimacy alone with her Beloved.

In her late works, Teresa introduces the theme of the empowerment and innate dignity of women through highlighting the perfection and ethical virtue which her nuns were able to achieve. She sees them as disciples and sees herself as the Apostle of God who wins souls for Christ while both being on a never ending journey to the heart of God.[134] She yearns to have her petitions on their behalf heard and taken seriously and this yearning ignites her texts. At the same time she is intensely aware of the dangers of pre-judgement already inflicted on her sisters. At times her despair is so great that she suggests that this may be true even in the heavenly courts. She wrote:

"Is it not enough, Lord that the world has intimidated us [sisters] . . . so that we may do nothing worthwhile for you in public or dare speak some truths that we lament over in secret, without your also failing to hear so just a petition? I do not believe, Lord, that this could be true of your goodness and justice, for you are a just judge and not like those of the world. Since the world's judges are sons

---

well—Feminist Perspectives on Spiritual Direction. New York. Paulist Press 1988 154-157.

[134] Teresa of Avila: Interior Castle 7 4 14

of Adam and all of them are men, there is no virtue in women that they do not hold suspect."[135]

Yet it is in her Foundations that her ethics of empowerment are most apparent. She wishes to lift up all human reality, and indeed human being itself, to reflect the experiences of love, mercy and compassion which she perceived in her mystical ecstasies. She opposes the harsh treatment of women with her communion with God in which she has learnt that women are to be loved, honoured and respected because of the love, honour and respect which God first bestows on them.[136] It is precisely through this divine love, honour and respect that women are worthy to take an equal place among men. It follows that failure to do so, or their being prevented from doing so, is a deliberate denial of the will of God for his children and that is a sin.

Teresa was always an astute social commentator, but did not confine her comments to the battle of the genders. She also critiqued her society in which love of money, prestige and power were regarded as the heights of personal achievement and sophistication. It may be argued that she did so because the worlds of money, honour and power were essentially masculine but to do so is to diminish and belittle her motive for doing so. Again she did not want

---

[135] Teresa of Avila <u>The Way of Perfection</u> 3,7,51.

[136] In response to the cultural preference for males pertaining at the time, Teresa extolled the virtues of women and the shame of parents who do not realise "the great blessings that can come through daughters or of the great suffering that can come through sons." Teresa of Avila <u>Foundations</u> 20.3 198.

*How to See a Vision*

the female voice to be heard in these places because it was female but because equality lies in Jesus' heart. The grace which eternally flows from it flows equally to all, irrespective of gender, class or task. In her vision she saw that ". . . lineage and social status mattered not at all in the judgement of God."[137] Even Christian families could not, or would not, see this. Teresa writes of women and girls who clearly had a vocation to the coenobitic life but who were whipped and punished when they expressed their calling or took steps to fulfil it. Some felt this calling so strongly that they physically disfigured themselves to avoid marriage. Punishment and self-abuse are symptomatic of a failure to see and practice the equality which Jesus set before all people at all times and in all places.

It is interesting that one of these women, Catalina Godinez, gave Teresa a new definition of lineage which passes from the gendered, material and economic to the spiritual. This not only reinforced what Teresa herself had learnt in her visions it gave Catalina a mystical experience too. In Foundations 22.5 Teresa says that Catalina was reading an inscription on a crucifix when ". . . the Lord worked a great change in her. She [Catalina] had been thinking about a marriage that was being sought for her, which was better than she could have hoped for, and saying to herself, "With what little my father is content, that I become connected to an entailed estate; I am thinking of becoming the origin of a new line of descendants."[138]

---

[137] Teresa of Avila Foundations 15 16 175.
[138] Carole Slade; Teresa of Avila as Social Reformer. In Mysticism and Social Transformation. Janet K Ruffing (ed) with a Foreword by Robert j Egan SJ. Syracuse University

In addition to producing the reform of the Carmelite Order and establishing seventeen separate monastic houses, Teresa assisted the conversos [139] by admitting them into

---

Press. Syracuse New York. 2001. 102. The descendants of whom she spoke were of course, her spiritual children in the Carmelite Order.

[139] These were Jews who had converted to Christianity, either through conviction or social expediency. Teresa was herself the descendant of a converse and was keenly aware of the social and ecclesial injustice they suffered. This sensitivity probably stems from the public confession which her paternal grandfather was forced to make in 1485 concerning his secret practice of Judaism. A number of important works on the Jewish influence on the thought and writings of Teresa have been written. Among them are Diedre Green; Gold in the Crucible—Teresa of Avila and the Western Mystical Tradition. Longmead. England Element Books 1989. Catherine Swieticki : Spanish Christian Cabala: The works of Louis de Leon, SantaTeresa of Avila and San Juan de la Cruz. Columbia. University of Missouri Press. 1986, Gareth Davies St Teresa and the Jewish Question in Teresa and Her World Margaret A Rees (ed) Leeds Trinity and All Saints College 1981; and Teofanes Egido; The Historical Setting of St Teresa's Life, translated by M Dodd and S Paine, Carmelite Studies 1 1980. In my private conversations with Julia Burton Holloway at the International Julian Symposium in Norwich, May 2013, she suggested that Julian too may have been from such a family—or at least had extremely close connections with those who were. This is, according to Burton Holloway borne out by Julian's direct use of the Hebrew scriptures without the mediation of the Vulgate.

*How to See a Vision*

the order on an equal basis as every other Christian,—their piety and suitability for the religious life.[140] Conversos were sometimes regarded with suspicion among existing Christians who were more than a little suspicious of their motives and anti-Semitism was deeply entrenched in Spanish Society. But by accepting their wealth and social connections, Teresa offered them and their families the religious consolation they sought and the opportunity of philanthropy through the foundation of religious houses and institutions.[141] A spiritual foundation now replaced the material basis of prestige and wealth and in such a way that it is possible to speculate that Teresa would have agreed with Julian that all our sufferings will be turned into honours.[142]

---

[140] Op cit Slade 100
[141] ibid
[142] LT 28 227.

# Conclusions

This study has shown that contemplation of the love of God, experienced in prayer and in visions, is not a private transaction between the mystic and God. It spills over into the world creating a coherent and distinctively Christian Ethical System which is radical in its implications and in fact.

Both Julian and Teresa envisioned a new social order in which all things and all people were equal and all equally capable of deification through an ever closer union with God. They both set in motion a revolutionary paradigm shift in the religious and social order of their day which eradicates the long held assumptions of the established order and undermine the traditions of wealth, rank and task. This was achieved through a fearless struggle to uphold the eternal truths taught by Jesus through the Gospels, the authentic magisterium of his Church and their own lived prayerful experience.

The ethics of intimacy and love of the world helped to exert a powerful healing influence on the wounds caused by this revolution in State and Church. Identification with the suffering face of Jesus inhabited their consciousness and enabled them to reach out to the spiritual and social pain of others. From this mystical unity they discovered God's equality of love as they reached out to uphold the ethic of loving the world into being. But deeper still, they confronted the primacy of dignity as an ethic that must become part of the social good.

In other words, for Julian and Teresa it was not enough to experience the heights of mystical union. All such experiences needed to become the means by which all that is inferior to it and the will of God, in them and in the world should be burnt away. In this way they bore the risk of the theosis of the world. The ethics of perfection, as the journey towards deification, culminated in a series of ethical initiatives through which they asserted a spiritual impetus for ecclesial and social reform, which must continue in our day too.

* * *

Richard Norton.
Feast of St Augustine of Canterbury
26 May 2013.